Praise for *Yes, Y...*

MW01062111

"Reading this book is almost like having a coach looking over your shoulder as you are building your company. It's like having access to someone who can help you make sure you are running your business in the way that will lead to the very best results."

—**Aaron Katz,** Franchisee, HomeVestors of America

"Should be required reading for anyone responsible for the survival and success of a business."

—**Joe Hartsfield,** CEO, Hartsfield National Aircraft, Inc.

"The Sandler approach outlined in this book is so much more than selling. It is a highly effective approach to dealing with other people—employees, family, customers, you name it. And it is invaluable to any small business owner."

—**John Holman,** Development Agent,
HomeVestors of America

"A powerful, practical resource for every business owner seeking to improve work/life balance."

—**Laurie Stein,** President, Crawford Group

"Great insights for any business owner who has struggled to balance the long-term strategic vison with the short-term tactics of running a business and generating revenue."

—**Richard Horvath,** President, TheeDigital

YES,
YOU CAN
TAKE A DAY OFF

YES,
YOU CAN
TAKE A DAY OFF

Escape the Nine Traps of
Growing Your Small Business

David A. Hiatt & Susan Hance Sykes
foreword by **David Mattson**

Paperback: 978-1-7370102-8-9

E-book: 978-1-7370102-7-2

To my parents, Harold and Janice Hance,
and my husband, Dewayne Sykes.
—Susan Sykes

To my clients, past and present.
—David Hiatt

Contents

ACKNOWLEDGMENTS

Thank you to the entire Sandler book team and to all my past and present clients who have helped me build a successful business—and take vacations.

—David Hiatt

Thank you to my husband, Dewayne, whose unwavering love and support makes sharing life together a sweet adventure. To my parents, Harold and Janice, thank you for your love, self-sacrifice, and constant encouragement. I continue to be grateful to my brother, Michael, and sister, Sherry, who both helped me start businesses. To Rich Reed and Joe Kirby, who taught me business acumen and to invest in people. To my good friend Joan Hatcher, who has been with me through it all.

Thank you to my Sandler Coach Brad McDonald, who shared his leadership story and the original Leadership Compass. To my Sander colleagues, especially Jim Dunn and Josh Seibert, who have shared your experience and helped me to grow.

Each of you has made a lasting imprint on my life and empowered my personal mission: To continue to be a force for good.

—Susan Sykes

From us both: Thank you to Lori Ames, who inspired the idea for this book. To Yusuf Toropov and Laura Matthews, who worked tirelessly behind the scenes to birth our ideas into words and stick to the schedule. To David Mattson, for his vision and inspiration to lead Sandler as the world-class organization it is today and will continue to be. To our clients, thank you, for the privilege of walking beside you and sharing in your success.

—David and Susan

FOREWORD

If you own your own business, you already know that it's all too easy to reach a place where you feel like you're in way over your head. The symptoms are not hard to spot. Maybe your business has hit a plateau that wasn't in your plan. Maybe you're just not enjoying what you do as much as you used to. Maybe both of those things are happening at roughly the same time. If that's the case, you may have thought to yourself, "I know that plenty of other people have launched businesses and made it past this phase I'm going through. It must be possible to get to the other side. Plenty of people have done it. How can I do what they did?"

Maybe you're asking yourself what countless business owners we at Sandler have worked with have asked themselves—what if there were a playbook for entrepreneurs and sole proprietors, a battle plan that could prevent them from falling prey to the most common mistakes, keep them from buying into the belief systems that hold most businesses back, and point them toward the behaviors, attitudes, and techniques that spell success? As it turns out, there is—and you're reading it.

David Hiatt and Susan Sykes have been there. They've each owned businesses. They've each closely studied and implemented the best practices for entrepreneurs embodied in the groundbreaking work done by David Sandler, the founder of our company. And fortunately for you, they've put together a playbook that works.

Study it. Practice it. Follow it. And both you and your business will experience a breakthrough.

David Mattson
President/CEO, Sandler Training

INTRODUCTION

Owning your own business is rewarding—and it can also be exhausting.

The authors work with many small-business owners, and many tell us they struggle with issues that make their lives more stressful than they should be. They tell us that they face challenges like:

- High peaks and deep valleys in cash flow.
- Difficulties creating accurate revenue forecasts.
- Lack of clear vision or direction.
- No repeatable and scalable framework for revenue generation.

- Persistent communication problems with employees, vendors, and clients.
- Too many lost opportunities.
- Eroding margins.

Many small-business owners report experiencing all of these problems. They tell us they feel like the business is running them, rather than the other way around. A common complaint that seems to encompass all of the danger signs you just read is: "I can't ever take a day off!"

Once, a new entrepreneur might have dreamed of creating a legacy. Now, they are facing a situation where they are the primary or only source of revenue. Fulfilling that obligation takes too much from their families and from their own quality of life.

We can't tell you how many times someone has said to us, "I need a break—but I'm afraid if I take an extended vacation, the business will suffer or even go under."

These business owners, in our experience, can turn things around. The coaches with Sandler have helped thousands of business owners do just that. But in order to make that turn-around happen, business owners must first recognize the reality of their situation, namely that they have fallen into one or more of the nine common misconceptions that cause burnout for business owners.

The Nine Entrepreneurial Traps

Passion Killers

1. The "Setting a Vision Is Just for Big Companies" Trap
2. The "Nobody Does What I Do Better Than Me" Trap

Communication Killers

3. The "Sales and Marketing Are Basically the Same" Trap
4. The "I Should Treat Others Like I Want to Be Treated" Trap

Revenue Killers

5. The "Selling Is All About Relationships" Trap
6. The "Ours Is Better, and That's All That Matters" Trap
7. The "We Don't Have to Sell Because People Call Us" Trap
8. The "I'm Not a Natural-Born Salesperson" Trap
9. The "Sales Is Just a Numbers Game" Trap

If any of those sounds even vaguely familiar, you may want to keep reading. This book shares insights and actionable steps that have helped thousands of small-business owners overcome each one of these toxic misconceptions by implementing a powerful, proven revenue generation strategy that:

- Smooths out and accurately predicts cash flow.

- Builds a repeatable and scalable framework for growing revenue.
- Defines vision and direction that others will follow.
- Bridges gaps in communication.
- Creates and sustains a healthy work/life balance.

The two authors of this book, Dave and Susan, have each owned a small business. We wrote this book for those of you who do as well. We wrote it because we believe you can recapture your passion, create the lifestyle and legacy that you've wanted from your business, and keep your work and home life in balance, just as we did.

All we ask is that you move through the chapters, keep an open mind, and be willing to try some things you have not tried before so you can create a result you have not yet created in your business.

Together, we will take an honest look at how you became a business owner in the first place, the realities of running a business, the importance of working *on* the business rather than just *in* the business, and the best strategies for communicating in a way that causes customers, employees, vendors, bankers, and others to willingly help you achieve your personal vision by enabling you to generate more revenue. In other words, we will look at how you can sell more effectively in your role as an entrepreneur.

In these pages, you will find the coaching you need to implement a proven, repeatable process for putting you back in the driver's seat, both in terms of your business and your life. The kind of mastery we're talking about won't happen overnight. It is a journey. But it will enable you to make the kind of transformation that empowers you to say, "Yes—I can take a day off!" without fearing that doing so will lead to a crisis in your business.

If you're willing to take that journey with us, turn the page.

CHAPTER 1

Burnout or Afterburn?

I t was a chilly Monday morning in early spring. The sun was beginning to melt the last of the evening's frost. Avery had been working at the kitchen table for hours, a pot of coffee and her favorite cup nearby, too excited to be tired.

Avery was working on her passion project—her new business. She was about to take the great leap into the world of the entrepreneur as a small-business owner. She had placed her unique fingerprint on her offering, created her value proposition, set up her business plan, and secured financing, and now she was ready to go. All she needed was a customer.

There was a lump in her throat as Avery prepared to reach

out to her first potential buyer. Her heart was pounding as she punched the number into the phone. But she managed to turn her nervousness into action. She was fueled by pure passion and commitment. She knew the marketplace needed what she had to offer.

Her first call didn't result in an appointment. Nor did the second. In fact, the first few days of outreach had their ups and downs, but Avery was unfazed. She knew there would be adversity along the way. She believed in her dream. She was ready to persevere through the obstacles.

On Day 4: victory! She set up a meeting with Mai, one of her past clients. Avery and Mai had a trusting relationship from Avery's previous role, and Mai was excited to learn about Avery's new undertaking.

That meeting yielded Avery's first customer. Time to celebrate! Now her idea was more than words on paper. Money had actually changed hands, and a new business was born.

Mai's project was successful. The engagement led to three enthusiastic referrals, all three of whom also became Avery's customers. Those projects led to still more referrals and still more customers. There were some *noes* along the way, of course, but the *yeses* provided enough energy and inspiration for Avery to overcome the occasional disappointments. By the time she hit the three-month anniversary of the launching of her new business, she threw a party to celebrate. She was having a blast. She was motivated. She was on a mission.

Soon Year 1 was in the books, then Year 2, and then Year 3. By the end of that third year, though, Avery noticed something a little unsettling. The sense of mission had evaporated. It had been replaced by sheer exhaustion.

As she began Year 4, Avery found herself wearing many different hats—some she liked and some she didn't. She was the VP of Marketing, VP of Finance, VP of Sales, Customer Success Officer, and Chief Executive Officer. And she had to empty the garbage and clean out the break room too, which seemed to make her Sanitation Specialist.

Avery was about to reach a tipping point. We call it the point of "burnout or afterburn." Let us explain exactly what we mean by those terms.

Burnout is a state of emotional, mental, and yes, very often physical exhaustion that is brought on by prolonged or repeated stress. Though it's often caused by problems at work, it can also appear in other areas of life, such as parenting, caretaking, or romantic relationships. Left unaddressed, it can destroy your business—and a whole lot of other stuff, too.

Afterburn is a term from aeronautics. It's what happens when a jet needs an extra kick to launch from an aircraft carrier, punch past Mach 1, or evade enemy weapons. In these situations, the pilot switches on the afterburner, producing a major jolt of thrust. There's a dramatic whoosh of flame, and a new, more urgent boost in the jet's trajectory. The jet heads in one direction, fast: straight forward.

Entrepreneurs inevitably reach a crossroads where they face a choice. One road points toward exhaustion (burnout). The other points toward renewal (afterburn). Avery was at such a crossroads. Her next choice would either push her into a level of exhaustion that would threaten the very survival of her business or propel her enterprise into the supersonic realm.

In order for her to make the right choice, it was important for her to understand how she might have gotten to this point. Entrepreneurs fall prey to nine classic traps. Each is insidious, leading to the potential burnout of both the business and the founder without the founder ever being aware of the risks being taken. But each trap can be overcome and avoided in the future.

When you escape all nine of the entrepreneurial traps, you enter a phase of your business's growth—and your own growth as a person—where you have access to a vast store of energy, inspiration, and motivation. That's the afterburner kicking in.

The Nine Entrepreneurial Traps

Let's look at the nine common entrepreneurial traps that drive business owners like Avery to the brink of burnout, and then let's focus on the strategies that will generate the fuel needed for afterburn so you, like Avery, can summon the boost of energy you need to propel your business to the next level.

As you read what follows, we urge you to keep an eye out for the factor that connects all nine of the traps. Each of them is rooted in a belief that doesn't match up with reality and doesn't support entrepreneurs. These are misconceptions that business owners often buy into, sometimes for decades, that hurt both the entrepreneur and the business.

What follows is a brief overview of each trap. These traps fall into three categories: Passion Killers, Communication Killers, and Revenue Killers, which, left unchecked, lead to burnout. We will look at each of these issues in much greater depth in later chapters.

Passion Killer Traps

Trap 1: "Setting a Vision Is Just for Big Companies"

- What is your personal vision for your life?
- What kind of leader do you want to be?
- What is your vision for your company?
- What is its mission?
- How does the company mission tie into your personal mission?
- Why do you get up in the morning?

- If you have employees, why do they come to work each day?
- What is the purpose of your organization?

These are big questions, important questions, questions that need asking and answering—and they are not just for big companies.

This Passion Killer is rooted in the belief that personal goals and dreams are not connected to company goals and that they not as important for smaller businesses as they are for larger ones. This is simply untrue. A business of any size without a mission or a vision is at a competitive disadvantage.

When Alice in Lewis Carroll's *Alice in Wonderland* asked the Cheshire Cat, "Would you tell me, please, which way I ought to go from here?" the Cat replied, "That depends a good deal on where you want to go." Alice informs the Cat that she doesn't much care about her destination, at which point the Cat points out that, then, "It doesn't much matter which way you go."

Alice then insists that she meant that it didn't matter to her where she went, as long as she ended up "somewhere." The Cat assures Alice that she's sure to get "somewhere" if she only walks long enough.

It's an absurd exchange, but it's also a powerful parable for business owners. Walking aimlessly through your own personal Wonderland hoping to end up "somewhere" is a recipe for burnout and a sure way to lose touch with your passion. It's not a very enjoyable trip for your companions, either.

As a business owner, you have the privilege of choosing your direction. You also get to choose who, if anyone, you want to accompany you on the trip. If you dream of being a sole practitioner with a handful of clients and a lifestyle business, that's fine. If your dream is to build a multimillion-dollar corporation, or for that matter a multibillion-dollar corporation, that's fine, too. Just be clear on what you want. Own it! These are, potentially, great choices, as long as they are emotionally powerful for you and as long as they connect to what author and inspirational speaker Simon Sinek calls your "big WHY"—a purpose or calling that inspires you enough to change your world, and the world around you, for the better.

Whether your business is just you, you and a few, or you and a huge team, your goals and dreams matter. You get to choose your goals and dreams, and you get to say why you are choosing to move in that direction. Setting a clear vision ensures that you are moving forward with purpose. We'll look closely at how to overcome this trap in Chapter 3.

Trap 2: "Nobody Does What I Do Better Than Me"

This is the disempowering belief that it's faster and more efficient to do something yourself than to teach someone else how to do it. This trap manifests in the business owner working too much in the business's day-to-day tasks without allowing sufficient, or any, time for strategic planning—that is to say, working on the business.

This burnout-inducing belief creates a decision bottleneck where everything lands on the owner's desk and a culture of learned helplessness flourishes. It's not where you want to live. We will look closely at how to transform this belief in Chapter 4.

By the way, these first two traps fall into the category of Passion Killers because they drain away the commitment and enthusiasm you had when you were launching the business.

Communication Killer Traps

Trap 3: "Sales and Marketing Are Basically the Same"

This is arguably one of the most dangerous traps for a business owner. It is similar to the following Trap 8: "Sales Is Just a Numbers Game," but it originates from a negative belief about sales or a confusion about the difference between sales and marketing. As a business owner, you must understand the difference between branding and lead generation and selling. If you aren't generating leads, aren't converting your fair share of leads into clients, or are somehow confusing the two roles, you will run into trouble. Knowing where you are at any given moment along the sales/marketing spectrum is a great way to ensure you're avoiding this Communication Killer. More information on this can be found in Chapter 5.

Trap 4: "I Should Treat Others Like I Want to Be Treated"

This Communication Killer stems from a sincere intention to be a good business owner, employer, vendor partner, and customer-centric entrepreneur. All of that is good. But those good intentions can backfire when they don't take other people's predispositions and preferences into account.

When business leaders assume that the way they like to receive their information is how everyone likes to receive information, there's a problem. The same goes for assuming that everyone likes to deliver messages in the same way you do. And of course, you need to understand that what motivates you as a business owner is likely to be very different from what motivates your employees.

A successful communicator learns to adjust their message to their receiver. They become a student of human behavior and, in time, a master in the science of communication. We explore this more deeply in Chapter 6.

Revenue Killer Traps

Trap 5: "Selling Is All About Relationships"

While it is true that selling does require the ability to build sincere business relationships, the purpose of a sales relationship is to conduct business. This is a professional undertaking.

There is nothing wrong with being friends with your clients and prospects. People do buy from people they know, like, and trust. However, that's only part of the equation. People also want to be heard and understood. That requires great listening and questioning skills, combined with guts. It takes guts to risk asking tough questions. Sometimes asking tough questions can make you worry that the prospect won't like you, but you have to learn to move past that worry. Posing tough questions is essential for making sure that your prospects feel heard and understood and for making sure you have the right solution in place, now and in the future.

This trap, along with the following two, are avoided with the strategies and tactics explained in Chapter 7.

Trap 6: "Ours Is Better, and That's All That Matters"

This trap is the belief that since you have a great idea, product, or service, everyone will see the obvious benefits to working with you and the market will seek you out. When business owners fall into the trap of believing that the only thing that matters is being "better," they often find themselves exhausted after a couple of years of trying to prove it to people. Your job as a business owner is not to convince others that your product or service is better. Your job is to help your prospects self-discover why they think what you are offering will solve their unique problems. This trap is an extremely common challenge for entrepreneurs launching start-ups. (See more in Chapter 7.)

(Note: Ruben, one of our clients, fell prey to this "ours is better" trap, and it nearly destroyed his relationships with his investors. We'll share more about how he overcame it in Chapter 10.)

Trap 7: "We Don't Have to Sell Because People Call Us"

Also known as the "referral only" trap, this Revenue Killer holds that all problems can be solved with branding, inbound leads, and referrals. All of these are important for business growth. But it is likely that, if you are reading this book, a person-to-person sales process needs to be part of the picture for you. Have you ever experienced being referred to someone, but then you decided to purchase from someone else? If you answered yes, you know that people buy for their reasons, not the seller's reasons. A referral certainly helps to build the "know, like, and trust" factor, but there's more to sales than that. You may know, like, and trust your 14-year-old, but no matter how good their "sales pitch," you're not going to give them the keys to the car.

We will explore, in depth, how you can avoid each of the above Revenue Killers in Chapter 7.

Trap 8: "I'm Not a Natural-Born Salesperson"

The "I'm Not a Natural-Born Salesperson" Trap stems from

a negative belief about sales and the stereotypical view that a good salesperson is always talkative and outgoing. In fact, a salesperson who talks more than they listen is a liability. Listening and building an atmosphere of trust and comfort are skills that can be learned. It is true that some behaviors are more natural to some than to others. To an extrovert, meeting new people creates energy, whereas to an introvert, it takes energy. That alone does not mean an introvert cannot be successful in sales. Just as a person is not born an engineer, lawyer, or accountant, neither is anyone a "natural-born" salesperson. You can cultivate the skills needed. For more information on this, see Chapter 8.

Trap 9: "Sales Is Just a Numbers Game"

This is the belief that if one creates enough activity, i.e., the right number of outreaches, conversations, and proposals, eventually a sale will close. This is only partially true. The right activity executed poorly or with a "this will never work" mindset will yield poor results. The wrong mindset can generate a snowballing effect that leads to crises of morale and cash flow. Chapter 9 clarifies this in more detail.

SUMMARY OF KEY POINTS

Get ready for your day off!

- Understand the nine traps that lead to burnout.
- Be prepared to identify beliefs that don't match up with reality and don't support you as an entrepreneur.
- Make a commitment to use the principles and strategies you find in this book to kick on your afterburner.

CHAPTER 2

Accelerating to Afterburn

In jet engine science, the afterburner is not designed for sustained use. It is meant to be used in short bursts because it burns up to three times as much fuel as the jet uses before it is engaged. When pilots need an extra kick for a critical maneuver, and they sometimes do, they engage the afterburner.

What does any of this have to do with generating more revenue for your business? Plenty. Your attitude—your afterburner—is a massively important part of the success equation. It is the oxygen for your internal fuel that sustains your energy and, when necessary, provides that extra kick to propel your success. But how do you engage your personal internal afterburner for the extra kick you need? Is it possible to tap into your emergency potential fuel reserve, kick into afterburner mode, and push through your own barriers by transforming your attitude?

Yes, it is possible. However, while the process for mastering this essential transition is simple to understand, it is not necessarily easy to execute—at first.

> "A typical jet engine uses only about half the oxygen it ingests, leaving a large amount of potential energy. The afterburner, which is a long extension at the back of the engine, combines much of the remaining oxygen with jet fuel, squirted into the high-speed exhaust stream from the engine's turbine, and ignites the mixture. The resulting blowtorch shoots through a nozzle at the back of the engine, providing a hard kick of extra thrust."[*]

Engaging the Afterburner

In aeronautics, afterburn requires jet fuel, oxygen, flame, and a pilot who is ready to throw the switch. Similarly, there are four critical components needed to engage our internal afterburner as business owners. Let's look at each of them now.

---

[*]   Benningfield, Damond, "How Things Work: Afterburners," AirSpaceMag.com (*Air & Space Magazine* online), July 2007.

1. Who You Are vs. What You Do

We'll begin our afterburner boot camp with a close look at a concept called Identity/Role Theory, or I/R Theory for short. This theory (first developed by psychologists, not salespeople) challenges you to learn to separate *who* you are (in other words, your identity) from *what* you do (your role).

Here is the big idea behind I/R Theory: You are more than the sum of what you do.

For example, you may say that you're a business owner, and yes, let's assume that's true. But stop and think for a moment. Is that all you are? Of course not. You are also someone's child, right? Sure. What else are you? Well, maybe you're a spouse. A wine buff. A tennis player. A jogger. You get the idea. There is a long, long list of things that you do. Everything on that list may say something about the things that you enjoy, but none of them really say anything about who you are.

The fact that you are a business owner says nothing about your intrinsic value as a human being. Neither does your being a wine buff or a jogger, and neither does your playing any of the other roles on that list. However, what you do is very much a direct reflection of who you believe yourself to be.

That may seem like a strange distinction. Allow us to share an example that will make it a little clearer. Let's pretend that humans have perfected space travel and you have been selected to be the first human to take a vacation trip to Mars. You are super excited because you know it's perfectly safe and you will be home before dinner. (Just go with us on this one.)

There's no room for luggage on the ship. And, oh, yeah, there's no room for any of your roles, either.

All your earthly roles no longer exist. It's just you walking around the surface of Mars without a care in the world (or the galaxy). On Mars, you are not a business owner, lawyer, engineer, parent, child—you are just human.

Here's a question: On a scale of 1–10, where 1 is low and 10 is high, what is your value as a human as you walk around Mars?

Think about that for a moment before you answer.

What was your answer? If you said anything other than 10, consider that there are, at last count, a little over 7.6 billion people on Earth and only one you. There has never been or ever will be another you. Think of just how rare and valuable you are. You are irreplaceable. Would you like to change your answer?

When we introduce this concept to clients, we often hear some variation on, "That's nice, but what does that have to do with success?" If that is you right now, that's OK. You don't have to accept this—just keep an open mind for a few more minutes. Deal?

Great. Now, on our scale, the *who* you are is your identity. Your identity as a human is always an "I"-10. Everything else is a role.

Your score in your roles may not always be a 10, but your score as a human being always is. Skeptical? That's understandable. With so many bad actors out there, it's easy to think, "No way are we all 10s." But remember, we are separating the "I" from the "R." That guy who cut you off in traffic the other day may have been a poor driver and may have needed a little work in his role as a communicator, but once you take the roles away, he is a human being and a 10, just as you are.

We are all 10s.

Maybe this will help. Think of some little person that you love. Maybe it's your own child, a child that you are very close to, or even a child you hope to have someday. Imagine that you are there the moment this child enters the world. The child has not yet contributed anything to society at large. If we were to ask you to tell us that child's value on a scale of 1 to 10, what would you say? 10! Of course!

Fast-forward a couple of years. That same little person is learning independence and having a bad day as a two- or three-year-old. They stomp their feet and says things like "No!" or "Mine!" Granted you may be frustrated and tired at the moment you hear this. You may feel like scoring that child at around a 2 on role performance. But if we asked you the same question about their value, you know what the answer would be, right? No doubt, still a 10.

The same would be true through the teenage years and even as an adult. Right? No matter what the role performance, this beloved child will always be a 10 to you.

Now, if you can believe that about that amazing little person in your life, why is it so hard to believe about yourself?

A person's view of their identity is shaped at an early age, often with good intentions from their caregivers. Parents want their children to grow up to be productive, healthy members of society. They say things like, "Be good in school," and "Clean your room." There is nothing wrong with any of that; in fact, it's good parenting. But it's also important to understand that, in early development, a child's brain begins to connect good performance with "I am good." Conversely, bad performance equals "I am bad" in the child's mind.

And that is simply not correct.

One day, when Susan's nephew Morgan was in kindergarten, she went to pick him up from school. He was normally very talkative and excited in these situations, but on this day he was quiet. When Susan asked what was wrong, he said, "Well, I'm sad because I got a red dot today."

Susan did not have kids of her own so she was not familiar with the dot system, but it was pretty clear that red was bad. Morgan explained to her that he hadn't been quiet during quiet time and that he had just wanted to play. Susan tried hard not to smile. Morgan clearly understood how he was supposed to behave and now felt bad that he was "bad."

But Susan said to him, "You know, we don't like that you got a red dot, but we love you."

His face lit up instantly with a big smile. He said, "You do?" Susan assured him this was true. Which it was.

Now, Susan knew Morgan's mom and dad provided a loving, supportive family environment and his teacher was kind and caring. No one was intentionally attacking his identity. That's the whole point. The messages that children internalize from those around them are subtle. Often it's the case that those messages get interpreted in ways that are not in a person's best interests.

Why is it so important to separate your "I" from your "R"? Learning to separate your identity from your role performance is the first and most critical component in switching on the afterburners. You can only perform as well in your roles as you see yourself conceptually. Your concept of identity always affects how you perform in your roles, but you must never allow your role performance to affect your sense of identity. Whenever you want to hit that afterburner switch, you should remind yourself, as often as necessary, to see yourself as you really are: 10 out of 10.

2. Comfort Zones

The second tool in the afterburner toolkit is comfort zones—and how to avoid them.

Let's go back to Mars for a moment. The number you picked when you ranked yourself on a scale of 1 to 10 represents your comfort zone, also known as your psychological position. In other words, this number reflects the way you typically expect to perform in your various roles.

There are three broad categories of psychological positions. Let's take a look at them now.

Psychological Position 1: The Winner Comfort Zone

Typically, a person in the psychological position of Winner will score themselves between 7 and 10. This does not mean they always win. It means that they expect to win and that they expect to perform at a high level. They know they will sometimes fail. They embrace that failure as a learning experience and, ultimately, as a means to success.

When the pressure is high and the game is on the line, these people want the ball. Superstar Michael Jordan, an NBA legend, famously missed more shots than he made. Throughout his 15 seasons he attempted 24,537 shots, missing 12,345 (50.3%).[*] When the game was on the line, was Jordan saying to himself, "There's a 50.3% chance that I will miss"? Of course not. He wanted the ball and wanted to shoot. He expected to make the shot. With six NBA championships and 32,292 points to his credit, he was right often enough to make the Hall of Fame.

Psychological Position 2: The At-Leaster Comfort Zone

A person in this position will usually score themselves between 4 and 6. They expect to be in the middle of the pack. Sometimes they will perform at a high level, but they do not

---

[*] Cary, Tim, "NBA: The 10 Players Who Have Missed the Most Shots," sportscasting.com, September 25, 2015.

expect to do that consistently. Their thinking goes like this: "I may not win, but at least I did not lose."

This At-Leaster comfort zone is based on a fear of success. This person will perform well enough to stay on the team and occasionally hit the game-winning shot or close the big sale. But just when it begins to appear they are on a hot streak, something always seems to happen to break the streak. At the critical moment, they sabotage themselves without realizing that's what they're doing. They miss the shot, trip over their own feet, or lose the sale. But really, the "something that happens" is that their comfort zone is being pushed. While winning seems good, it's different and uncomfortable, so they adjust their performance to remain in their comfort zone.

Psychological Position 3: The Non-Winner Comfort Zone

This is someone who expects to fail. Sadly, in our experience, a person who scores themselves between 1 and 3 has a Non-Winner's comfort zone. Such a person probably falls into one of three categories:

1. They don't understand or believe in the distinction of identity and role.
2. They enjoy the negative attention and seek out the victim role.
3. They are experiencing some deep emotional trauma.

None of those is a great place to be. If you find yourself here, it is your responsibility to figure out how to move your experience and your comfort zone up to a higher level.

Now it's time for a question. Of these three psychological positions, which one would you guess misses their goals the most often? The answer may surprise you.

It's actually the Winner. Think Michael Jordan! These people take a lot of shots. That means they miss a lot of shots. They learn from those misses and take more shots.

Winners set stretch goals for themselves—and frequently when they get close to their goal, they move the target further away. They enjoy the pursuit of the goal almost as much or more than achieving the goal. They are consistently top 20% performers.

Typically, the At-Leaster will take fewer shots and miss fewer shots. Usually, this is because they only have goals that are set by others. They are less likely to take aggressive action in pursuit of goals that are not their own. If they do set their own goals, they make sure they are "realistic" or "safe." If they achieve them, great. If not, no big deal—"...at least I still have x." It's important to note that we've known many At-Leasters who have high incomes. The thought process is the same: "I may not make as much as the top performers in my field, but at least I'm better than the people in the tier below me—and I'm comfortable where I am."

Non-Winners take the fewest shots of all. They usually don't even have goals. Or, very often, they've already determined the goal is unattainable, so their belief is that there's no need to try.

Your subconscious mind is powerful. It has set up these psychological positions to keep you safe and comfortable. When you begin to go outside the boundaries of perceived safety and comfort, your brain says, "Stop—that's new, and new is uncomfortable." It's all too easy to fall into that trap.

Now, here is the challenge. Most life experience teaches that role performance determines a person's self-worth, their identity. However, it's actually the other way around. It is your sense of self-worth, your identity, that determines how you perform in your roles.

If you can only perform in a role in a way that is consistent with your self-perception (and that is definitely the case!), then you must learn to separate your self-worth (identity) from your role performances.

When you embrace this knowledge, you gain the power to change your psychological position—and break through comfort zones.

3. Reset Your Comfort Zones

Now for the third tool in the afterburner toolbox. Do an online search for the term "comfort zone," and you'll find hundreds of books, articles, and podcasts on the subject. But what does the term actually mean?

Here's our answer: Comfort zones are best understood as the limits that Winners are willing to move beyond on a regular basis. Often comfort zones present themselves as a fear that's stopping a person from achieving some big dream or fulfilling some important ambition. (For instance: "No one will take me seriously because I am too [old/young/tall/short/whatever] for this job.")

The antidote to a comfort zone that is holding you back usually involves some kind of big move or adrenaline rush—like skydiving, climbing Mt. Kilimanjaro, or telling someone you are going to reach out to fifteen C-level decision makers—so there is some social pressure for you to do just that. Sometimes, big moves are exactly what a person needs. If that's where you are now, our advice is simple: "Go for it!" Jump into your adventure with both feet and break through whatever is holding you back. There is nothing wrong with that approach.

Think of a comfort zone as a thermostat for your brain's HVAC system. When you set your HVAC thermostat for 72 degrees, the mechanics of the system work to maintain that temperature steadily. If the outside temperature begins to rise or fall, the HVAC system will fight to keep the inside temperature a constant and comfortable 72 degrees. Adjust the thermostat a couple of degrees warmer or cooler, and the HVAC system will respond accordingly. The larger the adjustment to the thermostat, the more energy and effort are required to meet the new demand.

Let's assume for a minute that you've accepted the idea that your identity is a 10. (It is.) Your job now is to look at your roles independently. In the chart below, list as many of your roles as you can think of in two or three minutes, and then rank your role performance on a scale of 1 to 10, where 1 is low and 10 is high. It's important to note that 10 does not equal perfection, nor does it connect in any way to egotism. Giving yourself a 10 simply means you believe you are awesome at that role and confident that you always find a way to succeed in that endeavor.

We've included a few examples to get you started.

Identity = 10	Role	Self-score	Role	Self-score
	Friend			
	Parent			
	Business Owner			
	Salesperson			

If you are honest with yourself, you will probably acknowledge that you have room for improvement in one or more of your roles. The good news is that it is always within your power to reset the thermostat. The bigger the reset, the more energy it will take. Summoning that energy is possible if you recognize that it is your role improvement that you are aiming to fix, not your validity as a human being.

4. Move Forward!

As the saying goes, "If you want something you've never had, you must do something you've never done."

If you want to reset comfort zones, you'll need to reinforce good habits and replace ones that may have helped you at one time but are no longer serving you well. This is the fourth tool for accessing your afterburner. To use it, complete the following simple steps.

Identify three roles in which you scored yourself between 8 and 10. These are your areas of strength. What are some specific steps you can take to leverage your strengths?

Identify one role that you would like to improve. List specific steps you can take to improve in that area.

Commit to following your action plan in each area for a minimum of 90 days.

Re-evaluate at the end of 90 days. Assess your progress and reset your goals.

Setbacks and step-ups: It is likely that you will have some setbacks—expect them. Plan for how you will respond quickly. The more quickly you respond to setbacks, the more quickly they can become step-ups.

Guess what? After summiting your personal Mt. Kilimanjaro, your DNA hasn't changed. The name on your passport is the same at the summit as at the base. What has changed is your role performance, your self-perception, your comfort zone, and your ability to switch on the afterburners when you need them. When embracing that failure or success in your role performance does not change who you are, you can more easily accept the risk of failing and succeeding—and you can access a new and powerful source of internal energy when you need it.

That power comes from the choices that you make and the actions you take.

SUMMARY OF KEY POINTS

Get ready for your day off!

- Understand that you are more than the sum of what you do.
- Separate your identity from your role performance.
- Stay in the Winner's comfort zone.

CHAPTER 3

Success Begins at the Top

uccess starts and ends with you as the owner. The Passion Killer most likely to undermine that success, regardless of the size of your business, is a disconnect between your personal vision and mission and the mission and vision you pursue for the business.

This chapter gives you the antidote to Trap 1: "Setting a Vision Is Just For Big Companies." This trap is the belief that personal goals and dreams are not relevant to the corporate vision and are not as important for smaller businesses as for larger ones. Your people (whether that means you or 1,000 others) look to you for direction. As the leader, you must, as the Cheshire Cat reminded Alice, decide where you want to go.

For many companies, the investment in human capital represents a large percentage of the profit/loss report. Most leaders understand the importance of identifying the skills and qualities required for success in the various roles within the company. However, few leaders have invested much energy into identifying the skills and qualities they, themselves, must demonstrate in order to be an effective leader. Your ability to lead people is the single greatest determinant in the rate of return on your human capital investment.

It's commonly said that people don't quit companies, they quit managers. A recent Korn Ferry survey[*] found that in a good economy, the top reasons people changed jobs were boredom (33%) and cultural fit (24%). Both reasons fall within the purview of the leader. The leaders who people want to work with most care deeply about their people. They genuinely want their employees to be happy and productive at work and at home. They aim to both inspire and challenge.

By the same token, employees typically want to please the leader. They want to be productive and happy at work and at home. They care about success in the role and the company overall. Seriously, when was the last time you heard someone

---

[*] "Breaking Boredom: What's Really Driving Job Seekers in 2018," published January 2018.

say, "I'm going to take this new job, and hopefully it will be a complete failure"?

So where is the disconnect? If both parties desire to succeed and that success is dependent on mutual success, why do some of the "right" people leave—and why do the "wrong" people stay? We believe it goes back to a simple principle of connecting your personal vision and mission to that of the business and clearly communicating that vision and message to employees, clients, and the marketplace. Leaders, in other words, must learn to be easy to follow.

In her first role as manager, Susan learned this lesson in a painful way. She was excited for her annual review, her team was working well together, and the project was on track. Her manager, Jacob, did give her positive feedback and praised her accomplishments. She was feeling pretty good—until it was time to discuss opportunities for growth. That part of the conversation took her by surprise. Jacob explained that a standard part of the review process was to ask for input from her team. He said that her team liked her but that she was "hard to work for." Feeling puzzled and a little stung by the feedback, she sincerely wanted to know what she was doing wrong.

Susan: "What does that mean? Did I hurt someone's feelings?"

Jacob: "No, they like you, they just said you are hard to work for. You have high expectations."

Susan: "Do you think I expect too much? Do you think I should lower the numbers?"

Jacob: "Well, no, we need your team to hit the numbers."

Susan: "Do you think I am pushing the implementation team too hard?"

Jacob: "No, it's your responsibility to make sure the customer is happy, to keep the project on track, and to protect margin."

Susan: "Well, what should I do? How do I become easier to work for?"

Jacob: "I don't know—just try not to be so hard to work for."

Now they were both frustrated. Jacob sincerely wanted to help but did not know how to help. Susan thought she was doing the right things. She cared about her team, often putting their needs above her own. What made her "hard to work for"? How could she both be a compassionate leader and hold people accountable for meeting expectations?

Today, Susan says that fateful meeting with Jacob changed the course of her development as a leader—and she's eternally grateful to Jacob for that reason. As a result of that meeting, she became a lifelong student of leadership and business strategy. What she discovered was that there was a missing connection, a mystery to solve. She learned that "hard to work for" did not mean that she was a bad manager. It meant that, beyond the key performance indicators, her team felt it was difficult to know how she viewed success for their role. This was especially true in the areas often referred to as "soft" skills, i.e., communication, decision making, etc. That connection remained a mystery, until she met our friend and colleague Brad McDonald (also a Sandler coach).

Brad is a successful business owner and a former captain of a nuclear submarine in the US Navy. As Brad shared some of the concepts he used to lead his crew and hold himself accountable, Susan thought, *This is it! This is the "how to be easy to follow" guide I've been striving to put into words!* With Brad's blessing, we now share it with you.

The Leadership Compass

Brad's advice started with an example from his years of military service as captain of a submarine. When you command a submarine, you are the absolute authority at sea. You are responsible for the safety of your crew. As captain, you must have a clear sense of personal purpose, vision, and mission that connects directly to that of the company (in other words, the US Navy). Your crew must be able to perform their duties and make decisions that support the mission, even when you are not there. They must be able to look to you for purpose and direction when theirs begin to fail.

Part of your captain's duty is to prepare the crew for success under your command. How to succeed should not be a guessing game or a pop quiz. There are times when the leader must supply the purpose, especially when difficult times arise. You must communicate clearly in words and actions. Developing what Brad calls the Leadership Compass will help you navigate rough waters.

> Great leaders have clarity of vision, purpose, and mission, and they communicate that clarity to others in a way that makes them easy to follow.

There are a few simple rules you'll want to embrace as you create your own leader's compass. These guidelines are the foundation of everything that follows in this chapter.

1. Focus your compass on yourself first.
2. Keep your written communication clear and concise—no more than two pages.

3. If you don't mean it, don't write it and don't say it. People can smell a phony a mile away.

4. Be transparent and vulnerable. You might as well admit you are not perfect. (They already know that anyway.)

5. Share the *why* that makes you all come to work. Share it often. Teach purpose-first leadership to your team. Help them develop their own personal compass for themselves and for their department.

But wait. Suppose you're not quite as clear about that sense of purpose as you'd like to be? That's great! You are in a perfect position to implement your afterburner.

Compass Heading 1: Identify True North

Your first priority as a leader is to define your personal true north, your life purpose. Keep in mind your personal purpose, not your company's. We will connect the two later.

Defining your personal vision or life's purpose is the direct connection to your fuel source when passion wanes (and it will). This connection ensures you will have the resilience to persevere and refuel your passion and your inner drive so you can fulfill your "big Why"—your purpose. Every compass requires a true north, a reference point that guides you, allows for course correction and ensures you reach your planned destination. That's what you are out to identify.

> A clear sense of personal purpose provides the fuel to your inner drive that ensures you have the resilience to persevere and refuel your passion.

Fair warning: This is the hardest part. It may take you multiple tries. Be patient. The first time Susan tried this, her purpose statement was so lofty that she could not remember it. That was a pretty good sign that it wasn't ready yet.

The purpose and vision that fuels your passion and inner drive is, by definition, unique to you. It is what makes you do what you do. It's the reason you sacrifice, the reason you keep going when the going gets tough. Think of it as the reason you choose to get out of your nice warm bed on a dark, cold, wet Saturday and work when no one else is around.

On the surface, it may seem that you do what you do to take care of those you love or to achieve a certain lifestyle. There is nothing wrong with either of those things. But your inner drive probably goes deeper than that. You could take care of your family in any number of ways. The path you chose is connected to something bigger than yourself. What is it that draws you to care for your family and yourself in this particular way?

The series of questions below can help you discern your own inner motivations, with the final bullet showing what it all adds up to.

- How are you uniquely gifted?
- What life experiences can be leveraged to accomplish your vision?
- What is it about your vocation that is rewarding for you?
- Who misses out if you don't show up?
- What is your purpose or inner drive? What really excites you and gets you out of bed in the morning?

Here is an example from one of our clients, Jim, a financial planner:

- "I am gifted with understanding of trends and managing risk."
- "I grew up with three siblings, and both my parents were teachers. There was not a lot of excess money, but they always put a little away for a rainy day. When my father died unexpectedly, my mom had a lot to worry about, but paying the mortgage wasn't one of them. In addition to saving for a rainy day, they had purchased a life insurance policy that ensured we could stay in our home."
- "I feel best about myself when I am helping someone."
- "If I don't show up, another kid might have to move out of their home—or worse."

And here's his final statement of purposeful inner drive, what it all adds up to—the single powerful sentence that answers all those big questions for Jim.

- "I get out of bed every day to create a world where people's homes are secure even when life is uncertain."

Steve Jobs famously said, "I want to put a ding in the universe." What do you want?

▶ *Exercise*

Take a few minutes now and create a working document, in a notebook or on screen, and answer the questions below. See if it brings you to the same wow finish as the example—a single powerful statement of purpose. Do that right now.

- How are you uniquely gifted?
- What life experiences can be leveraged to accomplish your vision?
- What is it about your vocation that is rewarding for you?
- Who misses out if you don't show up?
- What is your purpose or inner drive? What really excites you and gets you out of bed in the morning? ◀

If you didn't immediately get to the wow finish, don't worry. It can sometimes be difficult to articulate the answers to the questions we've just shared with you. There are two likely reasons for this.

The first reason is that completing this exercise requires a great deal of self-awareness. You can start by enlisting the help of a few trusted advisors in your life by showing them your first draft, asking them how they see you, and getting their input on a second draft.

Another option is to take advantage of the various personal development assessments available to you. There are many assessments that can reveal areas of strengths and opportunities for development, such as OutMatch and DISC, both of which we recommend to our clients.

Whichever assessment you choose, keep in mind that any assessment is only as good as the honesty that you provide in your responses. It's important to ask the right questions when reviewing your assessment results. Some of our clients say, "That's not right," or "I'm not like that," when they see their results. The right questions to ask yourself in this situation are:

- When might this be true?
- Is this attribute supporting or limiting my success?

A second reason you may have difficulty articulating answers to these questions has to do with emotion. Passion, for instance, is an emotion. Neuroscience has taught us that the area of the brain responsible for emotion has no capacity for language. Therefore, when people try to put their feelings into words, it does not "feel" right. When you begin thinking about what ignites your passion, it is neurologically difficult to put this into words.

Keep working at it. You may decide that it makes sense

to work with a coach who can help you through the process. When you can clearly articulate what drives you, the right people (employees and clients) will connect with your shared sense of purpose.

Our encouragement to you is to continue to persevere. You don't have to have all the answers to the questions before you begin; begin anyway. There is a lot to learn in the pursuit of understanding what drives you. We will revisit this again later in the book.

Once you have gotten an idea about what fuels your inner drive, at least something you can work with to see if it sticks, you are ready to move on to establishing the rest of your compass headings.

> The Leadership Compass focuses on your personal vision and purpose. The planning process that follows focuses on business growth.

Compass Heading 2: Create Your Definition of Leadership

In this step, you will take a moment to write out your personal definition of leadership. You will make it no more than one sentence long.

In crafting this sentence, ask yourself: What kind of leader would you follow? What qualities are important to you in a leader? Who would you follow? It's OK if your definition is aspirational. After all, you are on a journey. Remember that if you don't mean it, don't write it. People can smell a phony.

▶ *Exercise*

In your working document, jot down a few words that come to mind for your personal definition of leadership. ◀

Susan's definition looked like this: "Leadership is the act of being followed, through a relationship of mutual trust, by individuals in the pursuit of a shared vision or mission."

Dave's definition is a bit different: "Leadership is setting the goals and strategies to achieve those goals in such a way that the team is willing and able to follow you in the pursuit of achieving those goals."

Either of these definitions could be a good model for you, or you may opt to go with something else. Whatever you write, though, remember: If you look behind you and no one is there, you are not leading.

The reason people decide to follow is also important to consider. As the boss, you have a certain amount of authority to influence followers because of your position. When the chips are down, you want people who will stick with you and rally together to overcome challenges. That can only come from a relationship of trust and shared vision. A crucial part of that relationship is explored in the next step.

Compass Heading 3: Identify Your Core Values

These are your personal values, not necessarily the ones posted on the company wall. The two sets of values must align, but they don't have to be identical. If you are just getting started, begin with your own values. Then repeat this step for the company you lead.

Take a few moments to identify fundamental beliefs that guide your actions. Your core values should set out, in broad terms, the standards that you will not compromise.

▶ *Exercise*

In your working document, list a few words that come to mind that reflect your company values. ◀

Now that you have some words that point toward your core values, let's make them actionable. Usually when we work with clients on identifying their values, they list words like "integrity, honesty, respect," and so on. These are great concepts, but on their own they are not actionable. Simply saying that you value honesty does not tell anyone how you will behave in a given situation. As a leader, it's your job to empower your people to take appropriate actions and make good decisions.

Your core values provide that guidance, even when you are not there. Here are a few examples to get you started:

Value	Action
Integrity	Do the right thing, even when it is hard.
Honesty	Do what you say you will do when you say you will do it. Keep the promises and commitments that you make to others and yourself.
Growth	Learn something new every day.
Humility	Admit when you are wrong and apologize.

▶ *Exercise*

For each of your personal values, list action steps that put those values into action. ◀

Once you have a set of clear, actionable values that drive your decisions and those of your workers, it's time for Step 4.

Compass Heading 4: Identify Your Operating Principles

Your personal operating principles are the highest authority or standard for you, yourself. They are the rules by which you conduct your daily life and evaluate your role performance. Unlike a value, an operating principle is a binary proposition, a yes-or-no question you can ask yourself on a regular basis. It's the checklist that you review every morning and at the end of every day.

For example, see this table.

Morning	Evening
I am fair and just	Was I fair and just?
I am approachable and in control of my emotions. You can bring me bad news. *Note: When people stop bringing you bad news, that's a sure sign of big trouble in your future.*	Was I approachable and in control of my emotions when someone brought me bad news?
I set the standard. I won't expect you to look sharper or treat our clients better than that which you see me do.	Did I set a high standard?

▶ *Exercise*

In your working document, take a few moments to create a table like the above and list some of your personal operating principles. You should have three to five of them. ◀

Once you have those in place, move on to Step 5.

Compass Heading 5: Identify Expectations/Commitments

Notice that this step doesn't say "expectations and commitments." The two are meant for our purposes here to be actually a single entity. Expectations are one side of the coin. Commitments are the other side. You can't have one without the other.

The expectations/commitments rubric is a two-way street. It includes what you expect from your team and what they are empowered to expect from you.

Let's say you want everyone to be 15 minutes early for work and ready to begin at the appointed time. You must show up early, too, and be just as prepared for meetings with your team as you want them to be. Too often managers who make a habit of rushing into a conference room or call at the last minute totally unprepared become upset when a team member does the same thing—not advisable or helpful.

As a leader, you will get what you yourself commit to. If you have an expectation of the team, you have to make and keep a parallel commitment to them.

Another example of a powerful expectation is a commitment to continuous growth. You might set an expectation of reading one book a month for yourself and your team. Maybe that's part of what it takes to be on your team. Just make sure you hit the same mark yourself that you set for others.

Commitments are the things that you are dedicated to upholding for yourself and that your team commits to as well. Another example might be that you are committed to the success of your team. You commit to providing them with the resources and help they need; they commit to doing the activities required to succeed. (This also falls into the category of mutual agreements, which we will discuss later.)

Expectations/commitments must go both ways. There must be no hypocrisy from the leader. Few things will undermine trust and loyalty like hypocrisy. Remember the rule: If you don't mean it, don't write it.

▶ *Exercise*

List some of your expectations/commitments in your working document. ◀

Time for Step 6.

Compass Heading 6: Set Your Priorities

Clearly communicated and written-down priorities keep you and your team on track. Emails, phone calls, client services, prospect meetings, internal meetings, meetings with the banker, attorney—the "to-do" list goes on and on. Many of these things are important, but not all are of highest priority to you as a business owner. If everything is a top priority, nothing is a top priority. With so many balls in the air, how do you decide which ones to handle first? If you are away on vacation, will your team know how to prioritize the activities that are the most important to you?

The fact that you've surrounded yourself with smart people does not guarantee that their priorities align with yours. Have you ever asked, "How are you coming on project X?" and in response heard some version of, "Not too good—I've been working on project Y"? If that conversation pattern seems familiar to you, you may have an issue of competing or confusing priorities. Both projects may be important, and there are only so many hours in a day. No one wants to be a micromanager;

likewise, no one wants to be micromanaged. Your job as a leader is to equip your team to decide for themselves how to set priorities that align with yours—and then set the guardrails within which they can make those decisions without you second-guessing them or criticizing them. (We'll discuss this guardrails issue more deeply in Compass Heading 7, but it is important to note here as well.)

There are four primary groups in Susan's company: sales, marketing, training/coaching, and operations/administration. When these teams are unsure of what task to prioritize, they know, based on their discussions with Susan, that their job is to ask three questions.

1. Does this activity, directly or indirectly, generate revenue for the company?
2. Does this activity, directly or indirectly, empower clients to generate revenue?
3. Does this activity, directly or indirectly, advance team members' personal and professional growth?

These questions are in order of priority. It may at first seem selfish to rank generating revenue as the #1 priority. Consider, though, that their clients hired them to help grow their business. Susan puts it this way when talking to her team members: "We must have a deeply held belief that the best thing we can do for our clients is to be financially sound ourselves. If we aren't financially sound, we will fail at helping our clients do the very thing they hired us to do, which is to grow their business."

Consider this common metaphor: Before every commercial flight, passengers are instructed to put their oxygen mask on before helping someone else. That's not selfish. It provides everyone with the best chance for survival. Put your own financial "mask" on first.

▶ *Exercise*

Prioritize your list of your expectations/commitments, making sure they are highly visible, clearly communicated, and continuously reinforced. ◀

Once you've written down your priorities, why not set up your own list of "priority questions," modeled on Susan's, right now? (It's OK if they're identical!)

▶ *Exercise*

Set up your own list of priority questions. ◀

Now, you are ready for Step 7.

Compass Heading 7: Know Your Nonnegotiables

People make mistakes. Most of the time these mistakes are learning opportunities. You do want to create a safe environment for people to fail. Failure is necessary for success. But mistakes, failures, or errors in judgment while the employee is working within clearly identified guardrails are not what we are talking about here.

In this step, we are looking at the list of nonnegotiables—a short list of serious boundaries that, if crossed, self-disqualifies a person from your employment.

There are some obvious things that should be on this list, such as illegal activity. Other entries may not be as obvious. Face it: There are some activities that might not be illegal but that definitely would be inconsistent with most companies' culture or values. Let's assume that you have a core value, for example, of inclusiveness. A nonnegotiable corollary to that, one that would self-disqualify a person from remaining on the team, could be repeated use of language that is disparaging or insulting to others.

That's just one example of things we've seen on the lists of nonnegotiables of clients we have worked with. What comes to mind for you? Again, bear in mind that something like, "Making a decision I wouldn't have made," is not a nonnegotiable, as long as the person is driving within the guardrails the two of you have agreed to.

▶ *Exercise*

Set up your own list of nonnegotiables. ◀

When you know your nonnegotiables, move on to Step 8.

Compass Heading 8: Know Your Personal Idiosyncrasies

Everyone has personal idiosyncrasies. These are the little things, that, while harmless, can be irritating to colleagues. Think of it like a "hot button." If a person pushes your hot button often enough, you are likely to say or do something you regret. Remember, we said earlier that people want to please you as their leader. Set them up for success by letting them know how they might push your buttons—and what they can do to avoid doing that.

Do you need coffee before you can speak coherently first thing in the morning? Do you get aggravated when people leave trash in the break room? These are not things that you would fire a person for doing, but they would make you frustrated. We tell clients, "You can't get mad at someone for doing (or not doing) something if you did not tell them they could (or could not) do it."

What idiosyncrasies about your working style should you share before someone pushes your hot button? There must be one or two.

▶ *Exercise*

Devise an honest list of your own idiosyncrasies. ◀

Once you know what they are, move on to Step 9.

Compass Heading 9: Personalize Your Compass

Now that you've completed the outline of the elements that make up your leadership compass, you want to personalize it. In order to point you toward true north and give you the afterburner energy you need when you need it, your compass must reflect who you are, your values, and your identity. If you always adhere to certain ethics, you can add something about that now. If you feel strongly about particular universal values, this is a good place to include them.

▶ *Exercise*

Personalize your list of what's important with individual aspects that are essential to you. ◀

Once you've created your first draft, share it with a trusted advisor or your coach and ask for feedback on these three questions:

1. Is it clear?
2. Is it concise?
3. Is it a good reflection of you?

Remember, this is not the place for others to insert their ideas of what you should or should not pursue. This is your compass. However, honest answers to the three questions you just read are worth listening to.

▶ *Exercise*

Take all that you've learned in the preceding exercises to draft a personal compass statement you feel comfortable with. ◀

After your revisions are complete, share it with your team. Remember, it's OK that you aren't perfect. No one is. People don't follow leaders who are perfect. They follow leaders who are transparent and sincere, who know where they are going, and with whom they have a shared vision.

> People don't follow leaders who are perfect. They follow leaders who are transparent and sincere, who know where they are going, and with whom they have a shared vision.

Every company's culture is created by design or default. Make sure yours is by design. Sharing your compass helps to shape a very specific culture within your company. It attracts people who share your values and priorities. Recall that the major reason people leave a company is that the company does not fit their culture or values. People are the most important investment you make as a business owner. You will want to attract and retain people who possess both the right talents and the right cultural fit.

Last but certainly not least, teach your team to create their own compass. Your job as a leader is to create more leaders. Everybody leads at some point in their life and also at different points. Help your team members become leaders who are easy to follow.

> Your job as a leader is to create more leaders.
> When you have good leaders around you,
> yes, you can take a day or more off!

Once you know what's important to you as leader and you can articulate that to your team, they know how to succeed in following you, and you are a leader who is easy to follow.

Now—Set the Direction

Now that you've defined how you will lead, it's time to set and share the direction for your company. Connect your inner drive to your company's vision, mission, and message.

A vision statement is bold. It describes the world as you want it to be in the future, not as it is today. Free yourself from restraints and limitations. Let's look back to our earlier example from Steve Jobs. Consider how his inner drive to "put a ding in the universe" connected to Apple's vision statement in 1980: "To make a contribution to the world by making tools for the mind that advance humankind."

Even after its founder's death in 2011, Apple continues to revolutionize industries and be ranked as one of the most valuable companies in the world in 2020. Many books have been written about Steve Jobs and Apple. He is a great example of the power of connecting your personal drive with your company's vision, mission, and message to the market.

A mission statement is action focused and describes what you do. It tells the world about your industry and what they can expect from your products or services. It's how you do what you do.

One executive team we coached was passionate about building a company where the employees and the clients could live independently. For their employees, they believed that building a fiscally sound company provided the ability to be financially independent. In addition to generous compensation packages, this company provided financial education to their employees. For their clients, this was more than a philosophy. The company provided prosthetic limbs. A properly fitted device restored hope and literally meant the client could live independently. Here's how this company phrased it:

- Vison Statement: "We envision a time when everyone enjoys the freedom to live independently."
- Mission Statement: "To empower independence by

advancement in education and innovation in the field of prosthetics."

Both the vision and mission statement were derived from the exercise earlier in the section on passion and inner drive that we completed with this company during our coaching.

1. What is your purpose or inner drive? What really excites you to get out of bed in the morning?

   Answer: Independence for ourselves and others.

2. What is it about your vocation that connects with your inner drive?

   Answer: Seeing a person regain ability that had once limited their independence.

3. How are you uniquely gifted?

   Answer: We are compassionate and mechanically and medically gifted.

4. What life experiences can be leveraged to accomplish your vision?

   Answer: Our education and work experience.

5. Who misses out if you don't show up?

Answer: People with the willingness and ability to be independent, but who are currently limited in some way.

It took many hours to boil these answers down to a clear, concise, and compelling vision and mission statement that spoke directly to the prospective clients and employees. You would only be attracted to work with this company if your values and culture aligned with theirs.

▶ *Exercise*

In your working document, draft or revise your company's vision statement now to reflect your purpose and inner drive. Be bold!

Then, draft or revise your company's mission statement to reflect how and what you do. Make it actionable! ◄

Once you have taken all the steps we have laid out for you in this chapter, you will have overcome the first, and arguably the most crippling, trap business owners face: not having a personal vision and direction and then connecting it to the company's vision and mission. When you know how to avoid this trap, you have eliminated the single most common obstacle to flipping on the afterburner switch when you (and your team) need it.

By sharing this with your team, you have laid the foundation for creating a culture of self-sufficiency and empowered your people to succeed at their task in your company. You have become easy to follow.

SUMMARY OF KEY POINTS

Get ready for your day off!

- Set your personal vision, mission, and purpose.
- Align that with your business's vision, mission, and purpose.
- Become a leader who is easy to follow.

CHAPTER 4

Don't Go It Alone

This chapter gives you the antidote to Trap 2: "Nobody Does What I Do Better Than Me." This is the belief that it's faster to do things yourself than to teach someone else how.

This Passion Killer manifests in the business owner working too much on the business's day-to-day tasks without allowing time for strategic planning. It is rooted in a dysfunctional set of beliefs that creates a decision bottleneck where everything lands on the owner's desk and a culture of learned helplessness flourishes.

Know that the only effective way to make the decision to delegate is to make your vision actionable with a plan. We have discussed the importance of having a clear personal vision and the importance of creating your company vision and mission so you can achieve your personal vision. This requires planning that is focused on achieving your company vision and mission. You will not generate revenue on a consistent basis without a plan. "Winging it" is not an option.

Many clients we coach struggle, at first, with effective planning. They want to create a solid business plan, but they feel overwhelmed when they're staring at a blank screen without knowing how to start. They lack a process to follow. So let's take some time now to examine exactly what goes into effective planning.

Seven Steps to Business Growth Planning

What are your plans to increase revenue? Plans need to be created after you have a clear vision of where you want your company to go. Your personal vision will always be the driver of your passion for the business. Once you know where you want to go, then you can create the vision and mission of where your company is going and what the company needs to do to get you there. If you have not created your personal vision, company vision, and mission, go back to that section in the book to complete them. Then, come back here to start planning.

Planning Step 1: Internal Company Analysis

First, take a serious look internally at your business. Make an honest assessment of you and your company by looking at your strengths and weaknesses. Your personal strengths and weaknesses are important because in many cases you are the company.

Strengths: Start by acknowledging what you and your company do well. Do not be modest. Write down in your working document you and your company's top three strengths. Warning: Do not get caught in one of the belief-traps we discussed earlier. Perhaps you listed strengths like a durable product, state-of-the-art design software, or ability to create custom orders. Be sure to include the reason you believe these to be your or your company's strengths, especially if you get great client or customer feedback. Congratulate yourself on having developed them but take some time to consider what you need to do to keep these strengths or what could happen to diminish them. If there is a chance that your company's strengths could be compromised, create a plan to keep this from happening.

Weaknesses: Knowing your weaknesses is as important as knowing your strengths. Continual improvement has been the motto of leadership programs for decades. When you constantly work to improve your company's weaknesses, continual improvement is the outcome. This is a never-ending responsibility. Create a list in your working document of as many weaknesses as you can think of. Then, we recommend that you first work on the three weaknesses that have the greatest impact on generating revenue. As soon as you improve one of those weaknesses of your company, you will shift another weakness into the top three priority category. Work on the next three, and so on.

Rename weaknesses as opportunities for improvement, and you will reframe your attitude to a positive perspective, which will affect your decisions. Let us give an example. Pretend that your current staff does not have the skill set to take your company to the next level. You can choose to see it as a weakness that is holding you back or as an opportunity to upgrade their skill. If you see it as a weakness, your solution could be to fire people and hire new people. If you see it as an opportunity, your solution could be to invest in training to make sure your team acquires the needed skill sets. You can view internal weaknesses and internal opportunities as one and the same.

Internal threats are a different situation. What is happening or not happening within your organization that jeopardizes or threatens the company's viability? Later, an external analysis will give you insight into external threats. What we are suggesting here is that you look within.

Author Dave provides a great example of this.

Dave had worked as a coach with a certain client for about a year and submitted his recommendations for future involvement to the owner, Paul. Dave had learned several things about Paul's company during that year. First, and most importantly, Paul was rather disengaged and seemed to be looking for the next big thing rather than focusing on building his current company. Secondly, the sales team was terrible. To a person, they had a negative attitude about the training and were unwilling to change. They believed that you had to spend a huge amount of money entertaining potential clients with dinners, drinks, events, and other not-so-professional activities. The third thing Dave learned was that the sales manager and marketing manager were the only two who embraced new sales skills when they learned about them and used them to produce real revenue generating opportunities.

The written recommendations Dave made to Paul were: 1) the engagement should not continue until Paul eliminated his internal weaknesses—a sales team that was spending his company into ruin; 2) he should keep the sales manager and marketing manager as the sales team and let the rest of them seek alternative career options; and finally, 3) Paul should sit down with Dave to get his personal and company vision into alignment. The last sentence of Dave's proposal was, "I will call you to schedule a time to discuss these issues."

But Paul never returned Dave's call.

About three years later, Dave and his wife were going to spend a nice, quiet New Year's celebration at the local city club's New Year's party. As soon as Dave and his wife exited the elevator, they ran into Paul and his party of about eight people, several of which Dave knew from training the company. Paul welcomed Dave and his wife as long-lost friends, insisting that they join their group and celebrate with them. As the night progressed and the consumption of adult beverages continued, Paul appeared to be a bit tipsy. At one point, Dave noticed his wife and Paul engaged in an intense conversation. When the conversation ended, Dave's wife motioned him into the hallway and said, "You are not going to believe what Paul just told me. First, he said he loved you! When I asked why, he said it was because he took all your recommendations, increased revenue and margins substantially, and sold the company six months ago for ten times what he thought he would get. He said you were his hero for being able to see what was silently killing his company."

A good coach will be able to help you see where there might be vulnerabilities that threaten your company. We urge you to take a hard look at the internal operations, processes, and attitudes that might weaken or threaten your company's growth or survivability. Perhaps a belief that business owners do not have to sell could be the biggest threat to your company.

Planning Step 2: External Market Analysis

Now that you have your personal and company vision statements, do a reality check. Do an analysis of the external environment in which your company operates. This should be an objective evaluation of current and future market factors that are most likely out of your control and that could affect your business. Define the reality within which your company is operating by looking at all factors, including economic, social, technological, and political. Be sure to include a competitive analysis of the competition in your industry and market. Often this task falls on the marketing experts, which means you may want to outsource this as a specific project. A well-done analysis of the external environment will alert you to any adjustments you would need to make in your company's vision for the future.

One of our clients is a worldwide provider of products to the energy production space. The company is directly impacted by legislative policies and natural disasters. Failure to plan for external changes in their market has the potential to be devastating for their company. We worked with them to identify strategies for adjusting their sales strategies to maximize revenue and limit risk exposure.

> When you constantly work to improve your company, continual improvement is the outcome.

Planning Step 3: Company Vision

After a good, hard look at the internal opportunities and external factors, determine if you need to adjust your company vision. Be sure your company vision is in alignment with reality. If you were to continue to manufacture Conestoga wagons after the transcontinental railroad was completed, your vision to become the "go-to" company for Conestoga wagons would become meaningless with the reality of the railroads. Planning Step 3 is that simple. Adjust your company vision if required.

Planning Step 4: Critical Priorities

From the work you have done in the above steps, identify the three most critical priorities based upon the opportunities or weaknesses that emerged. You may brainstorm a list of 10–15 things to work on, but the task here is to narrow it down to the three most critical priorities needed to move you toward your company vision.

The reason you want three is for efficiency and effectiveness. No one has the time or the energy to work on more than three at a time. Remember you still have the everyday tasks of running a business to complete. You can always bring up another priority once you complete one of the current three. When you focus on three at a time, you have a greater chance of accomplishing each one in a timely manner and you avoid another Passion Killer leading to burnout. (We hope that increasing revenue is always one of your top three priorities.)

Now that you have the top three priorities that will move

your company closer to achieving your company vision, what do you do with them?

Planning Step 5: Benchmarks and Goals

Establish expectations and measure the progress toward completion of each priority. Answer these questions: What is the impact on your company if you fail to accomplish this priority? What is the impact on your company if you successfully complete this priority? What are the quantitative benchmarks you can set to monitor your progress?

As an example, say your top priority is to increase gross sales by 100% within the next 18 months. This means you will double gross revenue. If you do not increase revenue, you have no chance of increasing production facilities, which will cause the company to stagnate and allow the competition to pass you. But if you do double revenue, you can afford to upgrade facilities and stay competitive. To accomplish this priority, what do you expect you will need to do? A reasonable expectation is that you will need to add another salesperson and get them up to speed within the next three months. Your next priority is to maximize your current production capabilities to ensure delivery of the increase in products you sell as you double your gross revenue. A third expectation is that you will increase your price but not so much that you are not competitive.

> Set priorities and measurable benchmarks
> and track progress toward goals. What gets
> measured and tracked is what matters.

Now that you have expectations of what it will require to accomplish each priority, the next step is critical.

Planning Step 6: Accountability and Action Plans

For each priority, create action plans, establish due dates, assign responsibilities, and allocate the resources needed (including time and money). Whether you are the only person to do it or you do this in a team, be sure to complete this step. But, do not over-complicate it. If you are a "solopreneur," seek the input of your advisors. If you have employees, be sure to include the key people in this process. Do not be afraid to delegate to your current team. If you are worried that they may not be able to handle it, maybe you have the wrong people and your top priority should be to hire people you can trust (more on that topic is coming up).

We summed this step up in one brief paragraph. In reality, this step will require you to take all the time you need to be sure you create the appropriate action plans for each priority. Think it through and be thorough.

Planning Step 7: Progress Review

Establish and adhere to a regular progress-review process.

Book weekly meetings, one for each priority, to meet with the people responsible and to hear their progress report. Do not miss these meetings. These reviews will give warning if problems are on the horizon or, pleasantly, can let you know if things are ahead of schedule. This will allow you to adjust the action plans and to do this sooner than later. Again, this is a simple paragraph, but completing this step will make a huge difference in getting you closer to your company vision.

Communicate to each participant in these meetings exactly what they need to come prepared to share—for example, progress on key priorities and action items, successes, challenges, and roadblocks.

> Plans, measurement, and actions lead to continual improvement. Continual improvement is a never-ending responsibility of a leader.

D-I-Y or Delegate?

So now we're back to our big question.

Do you continue to go it alone, or do you delegate? By now the answer should be clear. Delegation is a key trait of effective leadership. Even as a solopreneur, you will want a team of trusted advisors. You may choose to appoint a board of directors, join a group of other business owners, or hire a coach;

whatever you do, you'll want to focus on the highest and best use of your time and money and learn to delegate.

If you choose to add people to your team and delegate some of the responsibilities that are not the highest and best use of your time, you will want to create a framework for attracting, hiring, and retaining talent. It may take more time initially to teach others. Remember, as long as you are the only one who knows how to complete a task or project, then you're the one who has to do it. By learning to effectively delegate, you escape another Passion Killer and create an environment where everyone is functioning at their highest and best capacity.

Organizational Functions: Positions

We have asked you to spend significant time thinking about where you want your company to go and what you want it to be. We have asked you to identify your top three priorities and how you will accomplish them. Now, we ask you to process that company vision and create a brand-new organization chart of functions only. Answer the question: What are the functions that need to happen to get to your vision? Do this without thinking of any people or personalities you are working with now. Do not worry if it is a position or function you will hire or outsource.

> Focus first on what functions/positions
> you need to accomplish your vision before
> determining who will be filling the roles.

Have some fun with this. Get a supply of sticky notes of various sizes, as these will represent each function. The largest sticky note is placed at the top with the function of Owner, CEO, President, or Top Dog, you pick. This is the function of leading the company.

The next largest sticky notes should be for the key functions that would report directly to the Top Dog. These will be the functional things like accounting, legal, human resources, marketing, sales, and production. These are usually limited to five or six functions. Based on the product or service, industry, and market, these functions will vary from company to company. Use your sticky notes to add to your organization-function chart.

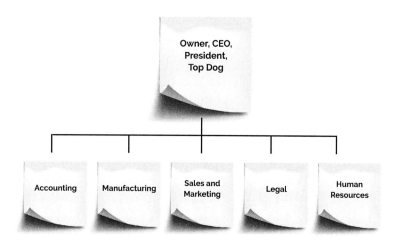

We recommended this exercise to the CEO of a growing company. The CEO had some fun with it. She realized (based on her planning, particularly the potential external threats) that she needed to add a whole new digital technology function to keep up with the constantly changing technology her industry was experiencing.

Now decide what functions are needed under each key function. Remember you are creating the functional organization chart that will get you to your vision. Your current organization chart may look nothing like what you are building now. Continue to think of functions only and not people who may be doing those jobs currently, and use the next smaller sticky note to add in the functions under each key function.

Continue adding the functions you believe are required.

Now for the hard part. Start at the top of your new organization chart and list what the complete, specific responsibilities and duties are for each function. Be as detailed as possible. Make sure that there can be no question as to what is required of the people who end up filling those functions. You want to identify the specific measurable behaviors for which the employee will be held accountable—functions and performance targets that can be talked about directly, committed to in writing, and signed off on, literally, ahead of time. This can be a time-consuming and difficult task. It is OK to get outside help from an expert. The ultimate goal in completing the positions information is to end up with a job description for each function, a guidepost for what needs to be done to accelerate your company toward its vision. This will give you a good idea of the functions you want to continue to do and those you want to delegate.

Organizational Functions: People

At this decision point, ask yourself, "Do I want to stay small and handle it all myself, or do I want to hire others and delegate certain functions?" You may have started a business by yourself, but it does not take long before you realize you need help if your business is to grow. To increase revenue on a regular, sustainable basis, most owners decide to rely on other people. You could be past this point and have already brought others on board. The question then becomes, "Do I have the right people in the right functions?" and "Am I utilizing my people at their highest and best use?"

Start with yourself. Which of the functions in your new organization chart do you currently perform? Maybe all of them. Which of these functions are you the best at performing? Which functions will you continue to perform, and which functions do you need to delegate to others by hiring people or by outsourcing?

Now that you know the functions required to reach the

company vision and which functions you will delegate to others, start putting people in those positions. Take a hard look at each of the people with whom you currently work and decide if they are in their highest and best use for the role. Match them to the required skills, experience, attitudes, demonstrated results, cognitive skills, and habits for the function they currently perform. If it is not a match, look to see if that current employee would be a better fit in a different function or if they should depart and find a job elsewhere to which they are more suited. These are tough decisions business owners must make. Remember, you don't help anyone by keeping them in a role for which they are not well suited. In fact, you may be holding them back by doing so and hurting your company.

Early in Dave's career, he was part of the ownership team of a large property and casualty insurance agency that was forced (an external threat that came to pass) to change the way business was being conducted. This required that certain functions be eliminated and that new functions be added. At the time, the company had 78 employees. When all the new functions were filled, only 36 employees were required. It took Dave nearly three months to decide who stayed and who left. Dave said the first three or four were easy, as they were going to be asked to leave anyway. After that it was extremely difficult. During this time, Dave lost 20 pounds without realizing it due to the stress of these decisions. The point of the story is that it is never easy to let people go whom you care about and with whom you have developed working and personal relationships. But for a business to survive and thrive, you will need to make these tough decisions.

Once all your current employees have been shifted to the new functions, which functions are left unfilled? Filling these unfilled positions could become one of your top three priorities. You may decide to outsource the accounting, human relations, or marketing functions. Whether hiring or outsourcing, conduct all the due diligence required to ensure the correct fit with the function you are asking the new person, hired or outsourced, to perform. The irony in this is that it may make sense to outsource help when putting current or new people into the correct functions.

Even though you hire a salesperson or a sales team, you are always the company's #1 salesperson. This is a function that you cannot delegate or outsource. Sure, you can delegate the day-to-day prospecting and selling duties to others, but you are selling something in every conversation in which you engage, whether it be customer, employee, or vendor. What you are selling is your company image.

> As business owner, you are always the company's #1 salesperson, even if you are not directly responsible for selling.

You are ultimately accountable for the outcomes, not just of the sales team, but of every working team that reports to you.

Many years ago, a client of ours, Don, was working for a delivery service. He had built up the business and was expecting a raise and kudos from the owner. Instead, he was chastised for some small mistake and was asked to sign a noncompete agreement. Don was upset and angry at the owner's attempt to limit his opportunity. He did not sign the noncompete—he quit and started his own delivery service. Not long after Don's departure, his previous employer closed. Don went on to create a large trucking company that is still doing well to this day.

Don became a successful entrepreneur because of his belief in himself, because of his passion for doing what was right, and because he wanted to be in control of his own future. Don did not buy into the entrepreneurial fable that owners do not have to sell. He was the only salesperson for his company for quite a while. Don learned to differentiate his role as business owner from his role as salesperson, and, as his business grew, he hired good salespeople so he could focus on working *on* the business rather than just *in* the business. But he also saw that many of the behaviors, attitudes, and techniques that had allowed him to succeed in sales had powerful applications elsewhere in his world.

Whichever emotion motivated you to start your own business, you may want to consider taking a lesson from Don: You are already in sales, whether you thought that was part of your job description or not. You are constantly selling your ideas and your business as a whole, to employees, vendors, bankers, and customers, even when you are not taking on the role of the "traditional" salesperson.

Effective leaders know that investing time in strategic planning is as critical to the long-term success of the company as the daily tasks of running the business. Effective organizational planning, combined with clear measurements and actions, empowers people to take ownership of success in their role. There will always be decisions that are appropriate for only you to make. By avoiding the "Nobody Does What I Do Better Than Me" Trap, you create a culture of self-sufficiency and empowerment—and another day off for you.

SUMMARY OF KEY POINTS

Get ready for your day off!

- Work with a coach, who will help you improve your delegation skills.
- Redesign your team's organizational structure by focusing on positions and people.
- Accept that you are already in sales.
- Empower others for a culture of self-sufficiency.

CHAPTER 5

The Sales and Marketing Conundrum

This chapter gives you the antidote to Trap 3: "Sales and Marketing Are Basically the Same." This Communication Killer results in poor messaging to the external marketplace and, internally, the confusion of two vital roles that are critical to the success of a company. The trap originates in one or both of two places: a negative belief about sales or a lack of clarity about the difference in the two roles.

Business owners play many different roles—and they have to shift from one to another daily and sometimes hourly. We sometimes like to call business owners who are spread too thin the CCB—Chief Cook and Bottlewasher. In start-ups and smaller organizations, they are often both player and coach, a situation that inevitably leads to problems.

In the CEO or leadership role, business owners are the guardian of the company's vision and culture. They ensure that all functions are aligned with the strategic directions by funding or defunding projects. As the chief financial officer, they must manage the financial resources. As the chief operations officer, they make sure the administrative functions run smoothly. Often in this role, they are also ensuring customer satisfaction, as well as overseeing delivery and implementation. Last, but not least, they are the chief marketing officer and the chief revenue officer.

With so many competing priorities, it's no surprise that one would want to combine functions wherever possible. A recurring mistake that we see is the lack of clarity between the marketing and sales functions.

Cori, owner of a law firm, considered attendance at community functions a "marketing" activity. She devoted a great deal of time to working on various committees, attending meetings, going on golf outings, and showing up at evening networking events. She was well-known and respected in the community. So we were surprised to hear that she was considering ending her membership in her local chamber. She shared that she had invested a lot of time, energy, and money, and her client base wasn't growing.

The week before, Cori had held three meetings with prospects that she had met through her work on one of the chamber committees. They had worked closely on the annual fund-raising campaign, so Cori felt confident she had good relationships with all three. Although each one was Cori's ideal client profile, all three meetings ended with some version of, "Great lunch, let's do it again soon." Cori shook her head and said, "I have a goal of three marketing meetings a week. I buy a lot of great lunches, but no business." When we asked, "Are you having marketing meetings or sales meetings?" she looked confused and said, "They are the same thing, right?"

As a business owner, you must understand the difference between the branding function and lead generation and selling. If you aren't converting your fair share of leads into clients, you might be confused about the difference in the two roles. There have been many books that take a deep dive into the different roles and executive functions of a business owner. The goal of this section is to drill into two of the most misunderstood roles and unpack why they so often collide.

Marketing and Sales Are Different

Although marketing and sales are different, both are crucially important to the success of your business. In fact, this is so important, it's worth repeating: Marketing and sales are not the same thing (never get them confused), and both are critically important. When the roles are clearly defined and working in lockstep, your marketing and sales functions can create a powerful team.

Not understanding the difference between marketing and sales is a fundamental problem. It usually stems from:

1. Negative belief systems about sales.
2. Never having clearly defined the two roles.

Negative Beliefs about Sales

Typically, business owners such as accountants, attorneys, contractors, financial advisors, remodelers, plumbers, etc., start their businesses because they have some educational background or skill that they have spent years developing. Whatever the skill, they are rightfully proud of their work and accomplishments. Often there is a resistance to saying they are a "salesperson"—just look up the word in your favorite search engine and you'll see why. A lot of people have had bad experiences with unprofessional salespeople. These unprofessional salespeople are often the butt of jokes and portrayed as selfish villains in movies. No one wants to be associated with that.

Consequently, many professional firms often refer to anyone responsible for generating revenue as business developers or marketers. They will say, "I'm a [lawyer/consultant/architect/whatever], I'm not a "salesperson." They practically hold their nose as the word "salesperson" comes out of their mouths. To make themselves feel better, they call it something else, like marketing, business development, or relationship manager.

A few years ago, we asked an accountant to create a performance-based compensation plan for our marketing manager.

He looked very confused and said, "Why don't you just pay her a commission?"

"Commission on what?"

"The business she closes."

We took a second to explain, "She's in marketing. How would we know which business was generated by her?"

"Don't you track who sells what?" he asked.

"Of course, but she's in marketing."

"Well, pay her a percentage of the business she generates."

It was clear we were not on the same page. Finally, it made sense—we were speaking different languages and we held different beliefs about salespeople.

Consider this: A professional salesperson is well trained in their products or services, as well as the craft of selling. They bring value that empowers their customers' success. They are willing to say no when the product or service is not the right fit, even if it means they don't make the sale. They wake up every day and face rejection and adversity because they have an unwavering belief that someone out there needs what they have, and it is their ethical duty to find them.

Every profession has its share of "bad apples." Somehow, folks are willing to believe that there are still some good apples in the barrel—except when it comes to sales. Failure to overcome a negative belief about sales can be a death knell to your business.

> A professional salesperson is educated in their craft, possesses expert knowledge of the industry, products, and services, and holds themselves to the highest ethical standards. Failure to overcome a negative belief about sales can be a death knell to your business.

Adding to the confusion between the sales and marketing roles is the overlapping responsibility for lead generation and growing revenue. Additionally, some of the activities involved in lead generation also overlap. For example, networking at a local chamber or industry event, making relevant connections on social media, or doing email outreach. Pretty confusing, right? How do you know where one stops and the other starts?

We'll deal with how to overcome negative beliefs in the "attitude" section of Chapter 8: Alignment. First, let's clarify when marketing ends and sales begins.

Marketing Role Defined

The American Marketing Association (2017) defines marketing as "the activity, set of institutions, and processes for creating, communicating, delivering, and exchanging offerings that have value for customers, clients, partners, and society at large."

Prospective buyers are savvy and demand that businesses speak to them in a language and methodology that is relevant to them. Marketing professionals are skilled communicators, often highly specialized and data driven. They are experts at engaging with the prospective buyer, in a relevant way, through the "journey from stranger to client/customer."

A "stranger" can be anyone in your sphere of influence. They may or may not be a prospective buyer. A well-crafted message to this group will attract individuals that may fit your ideal client profile to self-identify and engage with your message. In the beginning, an engagement might be a click, download, request for a call, etc. Once engaged, they become a suspect. Suspects look like your ideal client profile, they are within your industry, and they may purchase products or services like yours. When the suspect has reached a predetermined level of engagement, they become a lead.

The lead is the critical intersection where marketing activities and selling activities diverge. Until this point, your communications have been speaking to the marketplace from a one-to-many platform. For a lead to become a prospect, one-to-one conversation is required, also known as the "meaningful conversation." A meaningful conversation is a one-to-one communication with a person who fits your client profile and is the first step in the selling process.

> The lead is the critical intersection
> where marketing activities and
> selling activities diverge.

This conversation may or may not result in an engaged prospect. If not, they will go back to your suspect pool and continue to be nurtured by your marketing professionals. A prospect is someone who fits your profile and with whom there is an active opportunity to convert to a client/customer. Once a prospect becomes a customer, marketing professionals will continue to message to them in a meaningful but very different language than when they were a stranger.

> A meaningful conversation is
> a one-to-one communication with a person
> that fits your client profile and is the
> first step in the selling process.

The Prospect's Journey

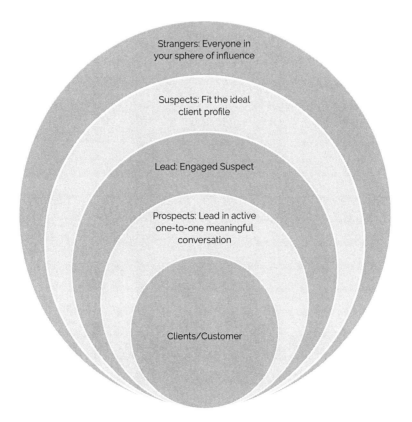

Sales Role Defined

Now to explore sales, as different than marketing. The primary role of a salesperson is to generate revenue. Many lead generation activities overlap both the marketing and selling roles. For our purposes here, though, all activities that precede the initial person-to-person conversation is considered "marketing," regardless of the role performing the activity. The sales process begins at the start of a meaningful conversation. Earlier we defined a "meaningful conversation" as the one-to-one human connection that begins the process of qualifying or disqualifying a prospect for the purpose of conducting business. Regardless of the outcome, the sales process starts at the first meaningful conversation.

> The sales process begins at the start
> of a meaningful conversation.

Earlier in this section, we met Cori, sole owner of her law firm. She was frustrated with marketing lunches that never seemed to yield any business. We worked with Cori to help her understand the difference between a "marketing" lunch and a business development (selling) lunch. She learned when to pivot and how to take the pressure off in both situations. Cori continues to have three business lunches per week, two that are marketing to suspects and one with a prospective client. Her practice is thriving. She continues to support her local community organizations and has a deep sense of satisfaction from her philanthropic efforts.

The key distinction between the two roles is the start of the meaningful conversation. Nowhere in the AMA definition of marketing does it mention "conduct meaningful conversations" or "close business." Those are two key roles of a sales professional. To escape the Communication Killer of "Sales and Marketing Are Basically the Same," you want absolute clarity on when you are the chief marketing officer versus when you are being the chief revenue officer. When you begin a meaningful conversation with a prospect, you move from CMO to CRO.

Create Your Message

In the next chapter, we will explore specific communication techniques that you will want to implement in marketing, selling, and any interpersonal communications to ensure that you are delivering the right message in the right way to avoid the next Communication Killer. In the meantime, now that we've detangled marketing and sales, we hope you'll agree that both are essential.

Salespeople need marketing, and marketing people need sales. Before either marketing or sales perform their role, you, the leader, must take a deep dive into who you are and who you want to speak to in the marketplace (see Chapters 3 and 4). Failure to do this step creates burnout in the owner and causes the message and the focus to become diluted for the business. As a result, the business will struggle to create its identity.

In these situations, decision making is typically reactive and near-term focused. It's difficult to attract employees when they don't clearly see how they fit into your future. The business may achieve a level of success, but it will wander to and fro, searching for its greatness.

The message you send into the marketplace matters. It's how you attract the ideal prospect and employee. It tells the world who you are and what they can expect from your company's products or services. It can be difficult to create a message that stands out from the crowd.

▶ *Exercise*

Let's play a game. Start a 3-minute timer. In your working document, list as many reasons as you can that a prospect should buy your product or service from your company. Give yourself one point for every answer you got in three minutes. ◀

We've played this game with countless clients. Most people get between 7 and 10 in three minutes. If you have 10, congratulations.

Now, the bad news. Look at your list again and deduct 1 point for every answer that your competitor could also say if they took the same quiz, i.e., integrity, customer service, industry expert, quality, local, relationships, etc. We know you are sincere when you say something like "great customer service or expertise," but so are your competitors. Really, do you think they wake up every day and go into the marketplace and say, "We have terrible customer service," or "We are dishonest"? Most people are down to very few or zero points at this point.

> If the competition is doing it, stop doing it
> right away and do something else.

How do you keep from sounding like everyone else?

Since you've already established your vision, mission, and strategic plan (see Chapters 3 and 4), turn your attention now to who you want to attract and build your ideal client profile. Can you close your eyes and describe them? Think beyond company size, industry, number of employees. Who are they? Where do they work and play? What do they drive? Do they own a boat? These are all clues about where to place your message and what to say to them.

Here are some other questions to consider about your company:

1. Is your company a boutique with high touch, or do your products and services have mass appeal?
2. Are you business-to-business or business-to-consumer?
3. Who within your target market is your ideal prospect?

Below are examples of interior design firms that at first glance seem competitive with each other.

Jill's interior design firm focuses on the residential market. She owns a high-touch boutique firm. Her ideal client earns over seven figures and wants to create a specific environment in which their home reflects their style. They want to be involved in the selection process but not the minute details. They do not have the time or desire to shop through all the options of fabric, paint, surface, lighting, and the list goes on and on. They prefer for Jill to give them a few options, select one, make minor modifications, and let Jill handle the rest. Jill's best clients want a turnkey service from design to delivery. Most of her clients schedule installation when they are away. They love the feeling of coming home to a "big reveal." Jill's firm bills the design as total package. Jill's clients establish a budget for furniture and accessories and purchase them all from Jill.

Nakia's interior design firm also focuses on the residential market. She too runs a high-touch boutique firm, and her ideal client earns over seven figures. Similarly, Nakia's clients also want their home to create a specific environment, like "for entertaining guests" or "a relaxing retreat." On the surface, it seems as though Nakia and Jill are both marketing to the same demographic. But look a little deeper and you'll discover that Nakia's typical client is highly involved in the project. They often want to contribute very specific ideas. They want to be involved in the details, with Nakia there to help narrow down the options to keep them from making design "mistakes." They love to be present during delivery and installation and watch as the whole project comes to life. Nakia's firm charges a fee for the design and the creation of the design pallet and charges an hourly fee for subsequent design meetings. Her clients often choose to buy anchor pieces of furniture or accessories from her and incorporate "finds" from other sources as well.

What does all this have to do with selecting the right type of messaging for your market? No doubt, Nakia's and Jill's clients have a lot in common, but they hang out in different places. Jill's clients are in and out of the local airport weekly. Nakia's have the financial means to travel, but their vocation does not require them to leave home as frequently. They are more likely to be season ticket holders for their favorite local sports team or symphony. If you are trying to engage them, you will want to take those differences into account. Just as both Nakia and Jill are likely to be found in different physical locations, they are likely to spend the bulk of their digital time in different online locations. A great message in the wrong place would be burning money—your money!

A great marketer understands more than just how to message. They know where your ideal clients hang out and how to reach them. They will collaborate with you to further identify your ideal profile—the more specific the profile, the better the results.

Note: Before you invest your hard-earned dollars in any marketing service or in any sales hires, make sure you've done the work to clearly identify your ideal client profile. One of the biggest mistakes business owners make is being vague about their ideal client profile. One successful marketing and advertising campaign for Las Vegas said, "What happens in Vegas, stays in Vegas." In both marketing and sales, "What happens in vagueness, stays in vagueness!"

To escape this Communication Killer, we suggest working with a coach or trusted advisor to work through this process.

SUMMARY OF KEY POINTS

Get ready for your day off!

- Accept that marketing and sales are not identical and understand the differences between the two.
- Identify and move past any negative beliefs you may have about sales.
- Make sure you've done the work to clearly identify your ideal client before you invest in any marketing service or hire salespeople.
- Make sure you know when to pivot from the marketing role to the selling role.

CHAPTER 6

Communicate Like a Leader

This chapter gives you the antidote for the Communication Killer "I Should Treat Others Like I Want to Be Treated" Trap. This belief stems from the dysfunctional idea that other people want to be communicated with in the same way you do. However, the fact is that often they don't. To avoid this trap, you will want to become familiar with communication tools and implement these techniques in your interpersonal communications, vendor relations, marketing messages, and sales conversations.

Buckle up! It's time to explore the neglected art of adjusting the messaging for the receiver.

Your Priorities and the Psychology of Communication

Here's some undeniable logic:

1. Generating income is top of mind for all small-business owners.
2. Your communication must always support the strategic priority of generating revenue.
3. If your communication does not support that priority, it is time to adjust it.

When you have conversations with potential customers/clients, the way you communicate with them has a direct impact on generating income for your business. Very often, how you say something is more important than what you say.

It's been estimated that facial expression, body language, and tonality can determine up to 93% of the meaning behind the words used in face-to-face interactions. If you want to put this to work for you, you'll need to learn that it is just as important to be aware of your facial expressions, body language, and tonality as it is of the words you say. Self-awareness of how your communication affects other people is vital to your success as a business owner. This book alone cannot make you an expert in this field, but it is our goal to make sure you understand how this can help you (or hurt you) in your pursuit of revenue generation.

We'll explore several key concepts in the art and science of communication:

1. Transactional analysis
2. The Karpman Drama Triangle
3. Pendulum theory
4. Communication preferences
   a. Behavior styles (DISC)
   b. Primary sensory dominance

> One of the best behaviors you can undertake as a business is owner is to read books on human communication and psychology. The more you understand how people, including yourself, think and communicate, the more income can be generated.

Transactional Analysis: Why People Communicate the Way They Do

Dr. Eric Berne is considered the founder of transactional analysis, TA for short. In his 1964 book, *Games People Play*, Berne lays out the basics of how and why people communicate the way they do. While TA proponents have authored many other books on the subject, our goal is to share the basics of TA to help you better communicate with clients, customers, vendors, and others as you generate and sustain revenue for your business.

TA continues to this day to be a viable explanation of human social interactions, or "transactions," as Berne referred to them. As we explore his thoughts, we will first discuss how you might be communicating with others and recommend options for better results. We will then share with you what can happen as the person with whom you communicate might be communicating in a less than desirable manner and how you can respond to make a difference.

As we begin, let us say this. We believe that all your business conversations should be honest and deal only with the truth so that everyone involved can decide what is best.

Ego States

Berne believes that people shift the way they are communicating based on how they are feeling and their state of mind. He refers to these behavior patterns as ego states. These ego states are a person's psychological realities. *Games People Play* says, "[A]n ego state may be described phenomenologically as a coherent system of feelings and operationally as a set of coherent behavior patterns. In more practical terms, it is a system of feelings accompanied by a related set of behavior patterns." Berne believed that at any moment in time, every individual is operating, including communicating, from one of the three ego states below.

Parent Ego State

In a manner of speaking, everyone continues to carry the voices and ideas of their parents or other authority figures around with them for their entire lives. This is called the Parent ego state. You might even have caught yourself sounding exactly like your parents, much to your amusement or consternation, depending on the situation. When that happens, it is obvious that you are communicating from your Parent.

Typically, the Parent forms in a person by the time they are six or seven years of age. Those rules become an endless loop in the subconscious, ready to spring forth in an instant. From your parents or guardians, you will have learned the rules of life, the do's and don'ts. For example, you can probably instantly fill in the blank, "Look both ways before crossing the _____." In fact, many people would have the answer by the time they read the word "both." This serves as an example of how quickly a person can transition into a particular ego state and how ingrained that early messaging really is. Whenever you are reciting the rules, making the rules, making judgments, or being parental, you are in your Parent mode.

Your Parent has two subsets. The first is Critical Parent.

Making judgments and being judgmental are two different things. When you hear yourself say things like, "What's wrong with you? Didn't I tell you not to do that?" or "Be good like your sister," or even something like, "If you were smart, you would buy my product," it's pretty clear you are communicating from your Critical Parent. Finger pointing is another great clue that you are in your Critical Parent. Also, whenever you say, "You should," "You ought," or "You must," look out—you are in Critical Parent. As you can probably surmise, this is not where you want to be.

One of our clients, Tom, shared this with us early in the relationship. He said, "My product will help my customers improve their production tooling's durability. What's wrong with these people who can't see that? It is so simple. They must be idiots not to see that." We suggested to Tom that his Critical Parent might be affecting his conversations with his prospects. We reminded Tom that he knew his product better than anyone else; after all, it was his "baby." Rather than being critical of their inability to make the connection, we suggested to Tom that he begin to think and communicate from his Nurturing Parent, which is the second subset of the Parent ego state.

Let's talk about Nurturing Parent. You are in your Nurturing Parent whenever you are being empathetic, helpful, or understanding. If you hear yourself say, "That must have been a tough situation," or "I understand how that can be difficult," you are most likely communicating from your Nurturing Parent. Just being there for someone to talk through an issue and truly listening to them is operating from your Nurturing Parent. You do not have to be talking to communicate. Listening is the other side of the communication coin and will often occur when you are in your Nurturing Parent.

So, back to Tom. When we suggested that he think and communicate from his Nurturing Parent, it was a foreign concept to him. Tom shared that he had grown up in a household with parents who were highly critical of everything he and his sisters did. They constantly reminded Tom and his sisters that they were not measuring up to the other kids in their parents' circle of friends. Whatever they did or accomplished was not quite good enough.

Tom had this Critical Parent script imbedded in him early in his life. Because he had experienced mostly Critical Parent, his "normal" became to communicate in the same manner. Nurturing Parent was not natural to him. Our first suggestion was to have him think of talking to all his prospects not as idiots, but rather as folks who just needed to discover a reason they would need to use his product so their production tooling would last longer. The coaching encouraged Tom to get into a nurturing, empathetic, and understanding mindset so he could help these folks discover that they needed what he was selling.

Generating revenue is the purpose of this book. To generate

more revenue, make sure 70% of your communication with customer/clients comes from your Nurturing Parent and 0% is from Critical Parent.

> To generate more revenue, learn to communicate 70% from your Nurturing Parent and 0% from your Critical Parent.

Adult Ego State

The Adult ego state has no bearing on your age. In the Adult, you make objective, autonomous observations without judgment or emotions and communicate in a nonprejudicial manner. Often it is described as "information in, information out." Every individual, including a child, is capable of objective data processing if the other ego states do not interfere. More mature people have learned to keep their Adult in control for much of the time as they communicate with others. This is especially true in business conversations.

The Adult is required for survival in this unpredictable world. It helps evaluate risks and determine probabilities, such as when getting from one side of the road to the other. In many encounters the Adult will act as the referee between the Parent and Child (see below) ego states. Communicating from your Adult ego state is vital if you want to grow your business.

When you communicate in the Adult, you are asking questions and listening to the responses so you can gather the right information to make smart business decisions. In working with Tom, we suggested he use the following Adult question to start a meaningful conversation: "So, help me understand, what is the lifetime of your typical production tooling?" We also coached Tom that his follow-up question, if appropriate, could be, "And why do think that is?" Tom reported back that these Adult questions were almost like magic. His prospects shared all kinds of information that made it much easier for them to understand how his product made sense for them.

To generate more revenue, Tom learned that 30% of his communications needed to come from his Adult ego state. For the record, that will work for you, too.

> To generate more revenue, learn to communicate
> 30% of the time from your Adult.

Child Ego State

So, if 70% of your communication should come from your Nurturing Parent ego state and 30% should come from your Adult ego state, that means 0% should come from your Child ego state. There is a good reason for this. The Child ego state is all "me, me, me," and "I want, I want, I want." You are communicating from your Child whenever you are emotionally involved and communicating from those feelings. When you are thinking or saying things like, "I'm happy," "I'm mad," "I'm glad," or "I'm sad," you are probably communicating from your Child ego state.

The Child ego state has two major components: the Adaptive Child and the Natural Child. The Natural Child can express in two ways: rebelliousness or creativity. Each of these Child components will result in a different emotional communication interaction. Remember, 0% of your communication should be from your Child, so this will just be a brief overview of each Child component so you can recognize them.

The Rebellious Child will engage in an emotional outburst to get what they want. After all, in a child's world, it is all about them. When a child learns at an early age that a tantrum will achieve the desired result, this behavior will continue into adulthood and allow them to become the drama kings or queens of the future. But an emotional outburst will not help you generate more revenue. The Creative Child will manipulate and figure out an innovative way to get what they want. Both Rebellious and Creative Child will tend to express spontaneously.

The Adaptive Child has learned to modify their behavior and communication based on the parental influence they experienced as they grew up. In this ego state, you either adapt to expectations of others or withdraw and whine.

There is no place for any of these Child ego states in a business interaction.

When you let your emotions control your communication, it will often result in regrets. You will say to yourself, "I wish I would not have said/done that!"

If your state of mind is filled with emotions, whether they be fear, excitement, anger, or despair, your mind will become clouded. You will respond emotionally. When you are angry with a vendor, an employee, or a prospect who did not buy from you, it is vital to do all you can to communicate from your Nurturing Parent or Adult. An employee may say, "You are a terrible boss who is just paying me as little as possible!" If this would cause you to respond emotionally because you feel you have given this person more than they deserve, take a deep breath, respond from your Adult, and ask, "There must be a reason you are feeling this way. Can you tell me why you believe this is true?" This Adult response will lead to a better outcome.

> To generate revenue, 0% of your communication should come from your Child.

The Karpman Drama Triangle: Handle Conflict, Avoid Drama

Stephen Karpman is generally credited with creating his Karpman Drama Triangle. He thought it better than the term "conflict triangle," but typically, when two people are experiencing conflict, it becomes natural to try to include a third party to mediate or reduce the tension that the conflict is producing; thus, the drama begins.

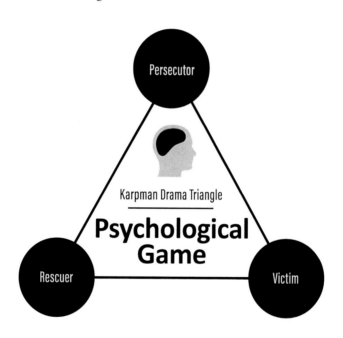

Karpman defined three roles in the typical Drama Triangle: the victim, the rescuer, and the persecutor. The victim will often feel victimized, like people are picking on them, like they are being persecuted, or like they are being deprived of an enjoyable life. The victim, full of negative feelings, will usually be communicating from the Child ego state with a "poor me" attitude. The persecutor, feeling superior, angry, and critical, is usually communicating from the (you guessed it) Critical Parent. When this dynamic begins to occur, often the victim will seek out a rescuer. The rescuer is more than happy to help. In today's terms, the rescuer would be called an enabler. When the rescuer is busy rescuing, it allows them to ignore their own issues. The problem is that this often creates "learned helplessness" in the victim. The rescuer can ignore their issues by justifying that they "at least helped" the victim.

The Drama Triangle is to be avoided at all costs. We bring it up to explain that many small-business owners find this type of dynamic occurring, not just in the business, but with family and friends as well. But the workplace is not the place to get your emotional needs met.

> The Drama Triangle is to be avoided at all costs. The workplace is not the place to get your emotional needs met.

When you participate in the Drama Triangle, you are satisfying an underlying emotional need, whether you are in the victim, rescuer, or persecutor role. When you feel others are attempting to manipulate you into the Drama Triangle, we recommend that you sigh (a great pattern interrupt—the conscious alteration to the pattern of communication the other person expects) and ask Adult questions.

The ability to understand, recognize, and control one's ego state combined with the ability to stay out of the Drama Triangle in your communication is an important step to avoid Communication Killers. These techniques open and conduct honest, straightforward communications that invite others to receive your message in a productive way.

Pendulum Theory: No Pressure Selling

Basically, pendulum theory helps you increase revenue without behaving like a traditional salesperson. Pendulum theory is the explanation of how you can help people discover that it is their idea to buy what you are selling. This applies to your products, services, or ideas as you interact with customers, clients, vendors, and team members. The concept here is to not look like, sound like, or behave as if you are a high-pressure, salesy person trying to convince them to do what you want them to do, whether it is in their best interests or not. Using the TA concepts discussed earlier, communicate in your Nurturing Parent and Adult in such a way that you stay behind the pendulum. Let us explain.

Pendulum theory helps you increase
revenue without you having to behave
like a traditional salesperson.

The pendulum represents the person with whom you are communicating. The rule is, "Never get between your prospect and where you want them to go. Stay outside the pendulum swing." Refer to the graphic below. Keep in mind that a prospect can be a client, employee, or vendor whom you are wanting to persuade to your product or point of view. Effective communication with each of those people above will help you generate revenue.

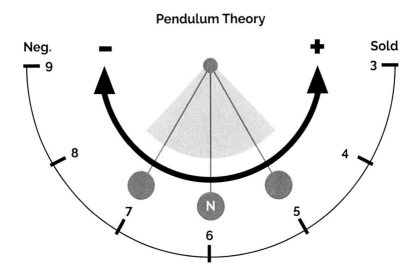

Pendulum Theory

Remember:
- Stay behind the pendulum.
- Never get between the prospects and where you'd like them to go!

Any person between 6 and 9 would be considered negative toward what you are discussing, while any person between 6 and 3 would have some degree of positivity regarding what you are discussing. Like a pendulum, the other person can swing freely between being totally on board (3: Sold) or being dead set against (9: Neg.) what is being discussed. Like a pendulum, a body in motion tends to stay in motion unless acted upon by an outside force. Anytime you get between where the other person is and where you want them to go, you become the outside force that slows them down or actually causes them to move in the opposite direction. Stay behind the pendulum!

When they say, "Wow, that is a great idea!" we want you to resist the urge to say, "I know. I thought of it." Instead, respond with, "I appreciate that. What caused you to believe it was a great idea?" Our hope is that you can see how the latter response keeps you behind the pendulum and will allow the conversation to move forward in a natural flow. The goal is to have a conversation between Adults, about the truth, so that both parties retain the ability to say yes or no regarding the discussion. That means they can decline to buy your product; it means you can determine that you can't or don't want to work with them; and either decision is OK. An important concept to help you stay behind the pendulum is to do your best to understand how and why each of you communicates the way you do.

> To stay behind the pendulum, do your best to understand each person's communication preferences.

Communication Preferences: Speak Their Language

Each person has their own preferences in terms of what they would like to experience when they interact with others. When you fail to recognize and adjust your message to the communication preferences of the receiver, it's like you are speaking a different language. But when you learn to speak their language, you escape the Communication Killer "I Should Treat Others Like I Want to Be Treated" Trap. There are a number of areas where these preferences play out, and it's important for business leaders to study and understand them. Here we will explore both DISC and Primary Sensory Dominance.

Behavior Styles (DISC)

According to the DISC behavioral model, most individuals behave in one of four broad, observable ways: Dominant, Influencer, Steady Relator, and Compliant. Each of these behavior styles depicts how that individual communicates with others and how they prefer to have others communicate with them. Revenue generation improves as you improve in your ability to recognize, understand, and adapt to the prospects, customers, and employees who will help you grow your business. This quick overview will help you understand the basics of behavioral styles.

> Revenue generation improves as your ability to adapt your message to others' preferences grows.

Dominant

"Let's go, let's make it happen" are watchwords for the Dominant. People with a Dominant behavior style prefer to get the big picture. Do not bore them with all the details. They tend to make quick decisions based on how fast it will get the job completed. Dominant people are not known for empathy and understanding, so small talk about how the kids are doing or how their golf game went holds little interest for them. They are task-oriented and not people-focused. Communication is to the point and assertive, and it must include what's in it for them.

Influencer

Socializing is what Influencers are good at doing. When a person's natural behavioral style is an Influencer, they like to talk and they like to be around people. Chitchat is a good thing to them. However, beware of too much chitchat. It can lead to rushed decisions because the time to get to business is taken up with the small talk. Influencers prefer to talk others into their point of view.

Influencers will make quick decisions. But rather than being based on getting the job completed (like a Dominant), it tends to be based on whether or not they think they will enjoy the outcome. High Influencers like to have fun, and they like to be liked.

Steady Relator

Peace and harmony tend to define the Steady Relator. A Steady Relator is a team player and is concerned with everyone on the team being heard and having input. So, before making major decisions, they will ask the opinions of the team or of others whom they respect or may be affected by the decision. They will work to get consensus. This typically means that the decision process is slower. Be patient as you communicate with Steady Relators to make decisions, and be sure to use facts.

A Steady Relator can do repetitive tasks and will tend to be the backbone of organizations. They like closure on projects and tasks and will work to get that done by nurturing relationships with team members.

Compliant

"Follow the rules and get it right" sums up the Compliant. Being task-oriented, a Compliant wants to know what it takes to get the job done or to make the "right" decision. They will analyze all data to arrive at the correct decision. The more information you provide to them, the happier they are.

As you communicate with a Compliant, stick to the task, provide data and facts, and avoid personal or humorous comments when you illustrate a point. They only want the information that will help them make the right decision. They will then analyze their data again—and again and again and again. The phrase "analysis paralysis" is at work with the Compliant. This results in slow decisions.

Primary Sensory Dominance

How people process information is important to understand. As you generate revenue for your growing business, you will be communicating with people of the various behavioral styles we mentioned and who process information in different ways. If two people are processing the conversation differently, it might seem like they are speaking a foreign language to each other. People tend to process in one of the three basic senses: visual (seeing), auditory (hearing), or kinesthetic (feeling). Each of these is called a modality.

Visual

Some people process information visually. This means information appears to them in images and pictures. Their mind is seeing the movie of the conversation. Even as a picture is worth a thousand words, the visual person wants to make sure you get the picture, which means they will talk fast.

When a person is processing the world visually, they will use visual words. They will say things like: "I see what you are saying." "Show me how that works." "Can you help me bring this project into focus?" If you listen, you will be able to pick up on the modality they use. This will allow you to use visual phrases, like, "Picture this," "Look this over," "What color would you add?" or "How do you see this working out?" Doing this helps you to connect with the other person in a way that makes them comfortable with you.

Auditory

When a person processes information in auditory modality, sounds and words are key. They want to hear what you say, and they want you to hear what they say. Choosing the correct words, using the proper grammar, and matching the rate of speech are important to an auditory. They want to make sure you understand them by hearing what they say. Words and grammar will fulfill that for the auditory.

Auditories tend to speak at a normal pace, with normal posture, and perfect enunciation. They will "hear what you are saying." Things will "sound good" to them. Great ideas will "ring a bell." Listen to the words they use to determine in which modality a person is communicating. As you pick up on the auditory words, it is important that you listen to what they are saying. As you are speaking, do not be surprised if an auditory person closes their eyes so they can shut out distractions and concentrate on what you are saying. A major disconnect for an auditory is when the person with whom they are communicating uses poor grammar, doesn't appear to actually listen, or says, "I see what you're saying."

Kinesthetic

"I feel like you may be a bit confused about modalities." You guessed it. Kinesthetics are all about feeling. As they process information, they think about it and let it roll around in their "gut" before they speak. They want to make sure you understand the feeling so you can get in touch with what they think. This means that a person in kinesthetic modality will tend to speak slowly from a laid-back, relaxed posture.

Slow down when you begin to hear things like, "Help me get my arms around this," or "I need to get a grip on the problem." When you begin to hear the emotional words or touch words, you are usually communicating with someone who is in a kinesthetic modality. Breathe deep and pause before you speak or answer questions. Share how you feel. Know that the conversation will take more time than with the other modalities.

> Learning to adjust your communication style
> allows others to become more comfortable
> with you. The more comfortable they are, the
> more likely they are to do business with you.

Congratulations! You now have the basics of adjusting your messaging to the receiver and escaping these Communication Killers. Apply them every day—it just takes practice to make them second nature.

SUMMARY OF KEY POINTS

Get ready for your day off!

- Accept that not everyone processes the world the way you are inclined to process it.
- Commit to determining how others process the world, and speak their language.
- Adjust to the modalities of others, rather than expecting them to adjust to yours. This will make it easier for them to trust you, interact with you, and do business with you.

CHAPTER 7

The 7-Step Template for Revenue Generation

More revenue will overcome plenty of problems for any business. Likewise, few things contribute to burnout faster than financial stress. When cash flow is plagued with peaks and valleys, business owners live in constant fear of taking a day off. A week off is out of the question. But it is especially critical to maintain a healthy work-life balance for the business owner. Believe it or not, the system explained in this chapter will give you the antidote for the first three dysfunctional Revenue Killers.

1. The "Selling Is All About Relationships" Trap
2. The "Ours Is Better, and That's All That Matters" Trap
3. The "We Don't Have to Sell Because People Call Us" Trap

Your Priority, Revisited

Let's begin with your #1 strategic priority. By this point you know what that is: revenue. Successful communication means having conversations that will allow you to generate more revenue for your business. Usually, this means conversations with people who can purchase your products or services, so the template going forward will focus on those types of individuals. But keep in mind the template and strategies we discuss can be used in the important conversations with suppliers or employees as well. So spread the word: These seven steps (developed by David Sandler) are the recipe to successful business outcomes in all areas.

We have discussed earlier how a business owner is often doing many tasks. This means that time is precious. Our goal is to give you insight and ways to be more efficient and effective when having revenue generation conversations. Simply put, we want you to sell more in less time. To help you accomplish this, here is our 7-Step Template for Revenue Generation.[*]

> Time is precious. Follow this template
> to sell more in less time.

Revenue Generation Step 1: Mutual Agreements

The essential first step when it comes to generating more income is to master the art of mutual agreements. The word *mutual* is important. To be a mutual agreement, all parties to the conversation must understand what it is to which they are agreeing and must have had the opportunity to clarify any uncertainties.

We believe that great selling is just a series of mutual agreements. There is an agreement to meet with each other, an agreement on an agenda, an agreement on next steps, an agreement on price, and eventually an agreement on whether to do business together or not. Between the multiple conversations, as well as during each of the conversations, there should be no surprises. The goal is to understand each other through the use of mutual agreements.

---

[*] Based on the classic sales tool, the Sandler Submarine.

Manage Expectations—No Surprises!

What do we mean by no surprises? We mean that all parties concerned should know what to expect. Here's a true story. Many years ago, Dave had the opportunity to work with a large global company. The vice president of North American operations, Victor, to whom Dave had been referred, wanted him to train 230 of their salespeople. Over a span of 14 months, Dave had worked his way through all the company's purchasing committees, and it seemed the higher-ups were ready to sign the deal. During the many conversations, Dave had shared and used the concept of mutual agreements and no surprises, which Victor liked and respected. On the Friday before Dave's flight to Houston to finish the deal and sign the agreements, he got a call from Victor.

Victor said, "Dave, I know how you don't like surprises. That's why I am calling. Don't get on the airplane Monday."

Dave said, "Why not?"

Victor replied, "Because the president of global operations flew in from Amsterdam last week and completely reorganized North America. I am no longer in charge of the sales team, most of the people on the training committee have been given early outs or fired, and there is a freeze on all spending."

Can you imagine how surprised Dave would have been had he showed up expecting to complete a multimillion-dollar deal only to be told it wasn't going to happen? Because he and Victor had been working together with the understanding of mutual agreements and no surprises, he was saved the cost and embarrassment of showing up for a lost cause. Had he showed up only to hear the news, not only would he have been surprised and disappointed, but there is also a good chance that anger may have intruded into his conversation. Mutual agreements are signs of respect for all parties involved.

No Mutual Mystification or Wishy-Washy Words

Along with no surprises, there is another rule: no mutual mystification. This ties into mutual agreements in a simple but powerful way. If you are not sure of what the other person means, ask. Get mutual agreement on what is meant. Wishy-washy words are a common way of creating mutual mystification. When someone says, "There is enough information here that we will give your proposal consideration," what do they really mean by "consideration"?

Once when we were on a sales call with the VP of sales, Steve, we mutually decided on the next step, which was to have Steve sit in on one of our trainings with another client so he could determine if he would want to put us in front of his group. We were OK with this and let him know when a suitable session was taking place—but warned him that the other client might want him to sign a nondisclosure agreement. We also told Steve that before he called this client, we wanted to make sure Steve would actually be there.

Steve's response was, "There's a good chance that I can make it."

We asked, "Does that mean 90/10 you're there, or 50/50?"

He said, "Well, 50/50."

We concluded, "You're not coming."

His reply, "No."

"Good chance," "fat chance," and "slim chance" can all mean the same thing: no chance! "Good chance" is a great example of wishy-washy words. Beware of others, like: "maybe," "probably," "we'll see," "possibly," "if it were up to me," "pretty sure," "odds are," and "under consideration" (which we mentioned earlier). We are sure you can add more to the list.

Clarification Questions

At any point in the conversation/meeting, it is OK to ask clarification questions to avoid mutual mystification. The question above, "Does that mean 90/10 you're there or 50/50?" is an example of a clarification question.

Clarification questions are a normal part of a conversation when someone says something that totally confuses you. It is natural to ask, "What do you mean?" To generate more revenue, clarification questions are critical. Most small-business owners do not have the time or resources to make mistakes. "Do-overs" for the small-business owner can be catastrophic.

Pretend that you own a design firm and just spent three days designing an office space upgrade for a client you worked with several years ago, when they moved into the original smaller space.

They told you that they had about $50,000 to spend on the upgrade, so you worked for three days to create a design of what they could do for $50,000. During your presentation, they tell you how wonderful it all looks but the price is too high. When did you clarify what they meant when they said they had "about" $50,000? You didn't. And now you have wasted three days of your precious time. You must clarify what "about" means. We will share more about this when we discuss the investment step a little later.

> Use clarification questions to avoid mutual mystification, wishy-washy words, and surprises.

Up-Front Contracts

When we teach people how to implement mutual agreements, we start with Up-Front Contracts. This is the creation of a verbal agreement up-front, in the beginning of a conversation, about what is going to happen or be discussed during the conversation and what the possible outcome could be at the end of the conversation. This up-front contract should always be expressed in a way that matches the other person's communication preferences that we discussed earlier and with a nurturing tonality, reflecting the Nurturing Parent ego state.

There are five key components to an up-front contract. We will discuss each one separately, then put them together conversationally.

1. Purpose
2. Time
3. Their Expectations
4. Your Expectations
5. Outcomes

Purpose

Why is the meeting or conversation taking place? When you can answer this question, you know the purpose. If someone says to you, "Let's meet to discuss the production requirements for the Valencia order," you know the purpose. When people understand why they are having the conversation, they will know what they need to do to prepare for the conversation and the topics. In the above example, everyone would know that production requirements are going to be discussed, so you would need to understand what product Valencia ordered, the quantity, the timing, and perhaps any miscellaneous details.

The conversations will be about many things, not just sales. If you need to generate additional margins and your production process is cumbersome, you could say to whomever is in charge of production, "We need to talk about how this process is working and come up with ideas on how to cut costs." The *why* of the conversation is clear. The purpose of the meeting is understood. All business conversations should be set up and begun with a clear statement of purpose. This will ensure mutual understanding and no surprises.

As we flash-forward to the meeting/conversation, the UFC will come into play. We would probably start the meeting with pleasantries before we get down to business and say, "Thanks for meeting with me to discuss the production requirements for the Valencia order." Always begin the conversation with the purpose of the conversation.

Time

The purpose of the meeting/conversation is usually confirmed when the time of the meeting/conversation is set to take place. You could say, "Are you able to meet for 30 minutes at 2:00 p.m. tomorrow to discuss the production requirements for the Valencia order?" When the other person says yes, you now know the purpose of your 30-minute meeting tomorrow at 2:00 p.m. To confirm your mutual understanding, you would then say, "Great, see you tomorrow at two to go over the Valencia order." This conversation simply set up the meeting/conversation.

Time is an important element in establishing mutual expectations for an up-front contract. When you acknowledge and confirm the time of your meeting/conversation, it is a sign of respect to the other person. How many times have you found yourself in a meeting that just drags on? If you are leading this type of meeting, it sends a signal to others that you do not respect their time. By default, it implies you do not respect them.

Tasks will generally expand or contract to the time people are given to accomplish them. If you are given two weeks to finish a project, it will usually take the entire two weeks, with most activity happening in the last few days. If you need to finish the same project in four days, you will most likely be able to get it accomplished in four days. When you attach time limits to your conversations, you have a better chance of accomplishing your purpose without wasting time on nonrelated topics.

At the meeting itself, this part of the up-front contract will again come into play. After you remind them of the purpose, you would say, "Are you still OK with 30 minutes, or has something changed?" If something has changed you can trim the agenda or reschedule to a time when the full 30 minutes is available.

Their Expectations

When setting expectations for the meeting, it is best to get the other person's expectations on the table first. This could be the topics they need or want to discuss, or it could be their questions or concerns. People have an inner need to be heard and taken seriously. When you take the time to get their ideas, opinions, or concerns on the table first, it shows them that you take them seriously and want to hear what they have to say, without jumping into the old-school leadership of telling them the way it is and expecting your authority or leverage over them to get it done. (By the way, we use the words *expectations* and *agenda* interchangeably. We use both to mean topics, question, issues, and concerns.)

Early in Dave's career, he was in a meeting with his boss, Mateo, and several others about an account he had brought in. Dave was selling radio advertising at the time, and this was the largest single buy of his young sales career. This account had agreed to a large buy and asked to get the most for its money. So, Mateo started the meeting with Dave and went right into where this account would fit into the run-of-the-schedule spot (the actual radio ad) placements, allowing for the greatest number of spots to air.

Dave listened to this discussion between Mateo and the traffic person (radio slang for the person who timeslots the radio ads) go on for about 15 minutes. He was young and didn't feel confident enough to interrupt. Finally, when he realized they were talking about 2:00 a.m. slots, he said, "But the client wants all drive-time slots." He was in error for not making that clear before the meeting. Lesson learned.

But here's the takeaway. Had Mateo simply asked Dave

up front if the account had any concerns or comments, Dave would have said that the client wanted the best available spots in the drive-times. There was a lesson here for both Dave and Mateo. Getting the greatest number of spots to air was not the client's issue; getting the highest number of listeners was their goal. You can waste a lot of time trying to discuss your agenda first if it conflicts with the other person's.

In the meeting itself, you can ask as part of your up-front contract: "So, what are the topics, questions, or concerns you want to make sure we cover in our 30 minutes?"

Your Expectations

Many times, the agendas of the parties coincide, but there will be times when they differ. Often, the topical agenda is set when the time is set. When you get the other person's expectations on the table first, you can adjust your expectations, if needed, based on what the other person expects. If they expected a general conversation and you wanted specifics, they might not be prepared. In a case like this, it is better to reschedule with a clear purpose of specifics for the next meeting. No sense wasting time.

To better understand the other person during the conversation, you will need to ask them questions. We believe it is important to let people know what you are planning to do and get permission before you do it. This includes asking questions. Keep it simple. Ask, "Is it OK if I ask you some questions to make sure I understand things fully?"

> People don't get upset with you when you tell them
> what you are going to do to them and they agree.

This concept applies to everything. If you need to take pictures, ask. If you need to see their financials, ask. If you need to tour facilities, ask. Let the other person know what you need to do, and ask them if it is OK or if it is a problem.

At the meeting itself, now that purpose, time, and their expectations have been confirmed, you can say, "I will need to get into the details of what you need our company to do, which means I will need to ask you questions and take a tour of your production facilities. Is that OK with you?"

Outcomes

Knowing where you want to go before you start will provide you with a target to hit. Rambling conversations with no predetermined outcome can be a huge waste of your time. Of course, we are talking about your business conversations, not the casual chitchat of bonding with others. Outcomes can be defined as the possible action steps to occur at the end of the meeting/conversation.

When you discuss the possible outcomes, up front, you ensure no surprises. When all parties know the possible outcomes, no one will be surprised when you decide on the next step. The outcome should have at least two possibilities: to continue or to stop. In a revenue generating conversation, the outcome could be to buy or to not buy your product or service. A third outcome could be what we call a clear future. A clear future is mutual agreement to continue the conversation with a clear understanding of what will be happening, who will be doing what, and during what time frame.

A good up-front contract will focus the conversation and allow for understanding of what is going to happen and what the outcomes could be. So, now is the time to put the five key components of a good up-front contract together into a conversation you would have with a person you hope buys your product or service.

> **You:** "Thanks for taking the time to meet with me to-day so we can figure out whether what my company has can help you."

> **Them:** "Sure, no problem."

> **You:** "When we scheduled this meeting, we set it for one hour. Is that still going to work for you?"

> **Them:** "Sure, that still works for me."

> **You:** "I appreciate that. What are the key questions you need answered or the important topics you want to make sure we cover?"

Them: "Well, I need to know a bit more about your experience in working with companies like ours, what the process would be, and of course, how much it is going to cost."

You: "Not unusual. Those are things that most clients ask. But before I can answer, I will need to ask you some questions so that I understand your unique situation and give the correct answers to your questions. Is it OK if I ask you some questions?"

Them: "Of course, I would expect you to."

You: "Thanks, I appreciate that. Typically, one of two things will happen at the end of this meeting: 1) what we discuss will make sense to you and we see a fit with each other, or 2) it doesn't fit and we shouldn't be working together. At any time during this meeting if you don't think we are going to be able to help you, will you please tell me?"

Them: "Yes, of course. I don't want to waste my time if you can't help us."

You: "Thank you. And would you be OK if I tell you that I don't think there is a fit?

Them: "OK, but why would you not want our business?"

You: "It's not that I don't want your business, it is just that we are not for everybody. If I don't think we can deliver what you need, I want to make sure you are OK with me letting you know. On the other hand, we could both decide at the end of our meeting that there is a fit. If that's the case, we can decide what the next steps should be at that point. Does that sound OK to you?"

Them: "Yeah, that sounds good."

You: "Great, let's get started!

In this up-front contract example, go back and identify all five key components. Can you name the purpose, time, their expectations, your expectations, and the outcome? Go back and identify any wording that would keep you behind the pendulum. Our hope is that your up-front contracts become conversational and comfortable. A good up-front contract should not put pressure on your prospect or you. We know that initially this process will feel and sound awkward. Practice, practice, practice! Be sure to get out of your comfort zone.

Management Tip: By the way, this is what it sounds like with a vendor, with a salesperson, etc.

Revenue Generation Step 2: Compelling Emotional Reasons

People buy for their reasons, not yours.

To generate more revenue, help people understand their compelling reason to buy your product or service. It is not about how great you, your company, and your product or services are, rather whether your product or service will solve the prospect's problems.

There are only two reasons for people to make the decisions they make. Humans are that simple. Humans avoid pain or discomfort or seek pleasure or gain. Regardless of what product or service your company provides, it must help your customers avoid pain or provide gain. Compelling reasons to buy come in four flavors:

- Pain/Discomfort Now
- Pain/Discomfort in the Future
- Gain/Pleasure Now
- Gain/Pleasure in the Future

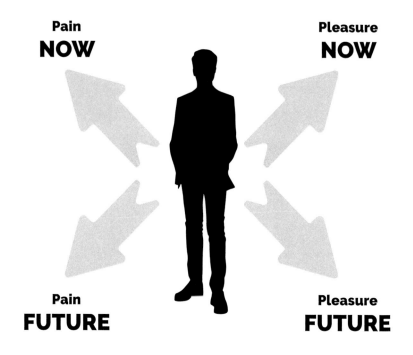

Pain Now is the most compelling emotional reason to buy. If someone just burned their hand on a hot stove and you sell burn ointment, they don't ask you about the ingredients or how long you've been in business or how much it costs. If their hand is burning now and you have burn ointment, they say, "I'll take it!" If you want to generate more revenue, learn how to get mutual agreement on the prospect's compelling emotional reasons. Because Pain Now is the most compelling, we will start explaining how to direct the conversation so the prospect discovers their true compelling reason to buy your product or service.

A problem, issue, concern, or opportunity is the first requirement to uncover pain (compelling emotional reason to do business). The problem the prospect brings to you is rarely the real problem. Here is an example: Henri, the CFO of a large regional manufacturing company, is seeking to hire a lawyer.

Henri: "I am not feeling too confident in my position at work."

Lawyer: "Why do you think that is?"

Henri: "Well, there seems to be some money missing."

Lawyer: "When you say 'some' money, how much are we talking about?"

Henri: "I think we are looking for about $88,000."

Lawyer: "You're the CFO; what have you done to find it?"

Henri: "We have conducted an internal audit and could not find a trace of it!"

Lawyer: "So, have you given up looking?"

Henri: "No. The CEO is so upset that she has asked an outside auditing firm to come in starting Monday. My guess is that by Monday afternoon, they will realize that I have taken it and gambled it all away. I am going to lose my job and go to prison!"

What was the problem Henri brought to the lawyer? He wasn't feeling confident in keeping his job. What was the real problem? He was an embezzler! The impact on Henri was losing his job and going to prison. Getting to the real problem and the impact is like putting together a three-piece pain puzzle.

The puzzle recognizes the intellectual requirement of pain. But remember pain is the person's compelling emotional reason to buy your product or service. Emotions are the glue that complete the pain puzzle and hold it together. If there is no emotional connection to the impact, there will not be enough pain with just the three intellectual pieces. How do they really feel about experiencing the impact of the real problem (the reason)? This is the question that will lead you to generate more revenue.

To help put this puzzle together and to help you find real pain, Sandler has a tool called the Sandler Pain Funnel®. This gives you a template for asking questions in such a way that the prospect can discover their compelling emotional reason to buy your product or service. The key thing to remember is that it is the answers to the Pain Funnel questions that are important, not necessarily the literal words you use to ask the questions. We have seen many people think they have to ask the exact question in the exact order to find pain. That will usually sound anything but conversational. Let's talk about the questions one by one.

Sandler Pain Funnel

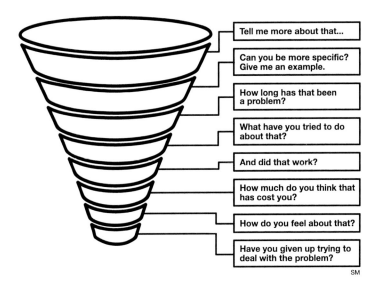

Tell me more about that...

Can you be more specific? Give me an example.

How long has that been a problem?

What have you tried to do about that?

And did that work?

How much do you think that has cost you?

How do you feel about that?

Have you given up trying to deal with the problem?

SM

The first request in the Pain Funnel is, "Tell me more." How many ways can you ask for information? "What happened?" "So, what is going on?" "What else can you tell me?" You get the idea; there are many ways to ask for more information when customers, prospects, employees, or vendors come to you with a problem, issue, concern, or opportunity. Get the Pain Funnel started by asking for more information, and make sure you listen and take notes. It is OK to ask clarification questions as they explain. In fact, sometimes they share so much you will already gather the answers to the next three questions without ever having to ask. Pay attention and ask the appropriate question as they share the information.

In the case where the other person has not provided enough information, you can move down the Pain Funnel and ask, "Can you be more specific or give me an example?" The purpose is to gather as much detail about their situation as you are able. When they start thinking of the details, it puts their brain in a position to recall all the reasons they are not happy with their current situation. Even though we call it the Pain Funnel, remember, they could be seeking gain. The conversation will remind them of all the reasons why you could help them.

"How long has that been a problem?" Getting the answer to this question is critical. If the situation has been around for years, why take care of it now? What changed to make this critical now? If it has been going on for years, they may have become numb to the true impact and learned to live with it. If they have just experienced the problem, they may not have had enough time to understand the full impact it has or will have on them. Just getting an answer is not enough. You need to ask additional *why* questions to truly understand the effect time has had in contributing to the issue you are discussing.

These first few questions of Pain Funnel usually lead you to uncover the real problem, the reason for their initial concern. As you get them to talk about the details and specifics of their situation, you help them discover the breadth and depth of the issue. Your next step is to help them begin to understand the impact, how this is affecting them or their company, and sometimes both.

"What have you tried to do about it?" What you want to discover in the answer to this question is what they have already attempted to do to fix the problem. You don't want to be making the same recommendation that they have already tried. This question could be asked straight up. It makes sense to ask, "What have you tried already?" or "What have you already done to fix it?"

Sometimes you can ask multiple-choice or presumptive questions. A multiple-choice question is when you give them more than one option of things they could have done and ask if they have done any one or more of them. This is a great way to subliminally demonstrate your experience and expertise. The fact that you know what the different options are will imply that you have knowledge. It might sound like this: "Before, when people have come to us with this problem, they usually have already asked their current supplier to fix the problem or they have tried to fix it themselves. Which have you tried?" Of course, the options you would provide should be situationally appropriate and reasonable as common ways to fix the problem being discussed.

Presumptive questions assume they have tried the common methods of fixing the problem. You presume they did what they should have done. "When you called your current web designer to fix this for you, what did they say?" Be aware of your tonality and facial expressions when you ask these questions. You do not want to come off as a know-it-all. You want to appear sincerely concerned.

Asking the above kinds of questions and digging into what they have already tried will usually include them describing what they did. If they don't tell you why it didn't work, you will have to get the answer to the next Pain Funnel question.

"And did that work?" If you ask this question literally, you run the risk of sounding a bit uninformed. Obviously, it didn't work, or they wouldn't be talking to you. You want them to acknowledge that it didn't work and to discover the reasons why it didn't work. Using the example above, if you ask, "When you called your current web designer to fix the problem, what did they say?" they may respond with, "They said they couldn't do it." Don't be satisfied with a simple answer—dig deeper. Ask, "Did they say why they couldn't?" As you listen to the answers, you are gathering vital information about a competitor and helping the prospect eliminate the current supplier as an option for them to use to fix the problem. You might hear how the current supplier has tried three times to fix the issue only to fail each time.

After hearing what they have tried to do to fix it, my favorite question at this point of the Pain Funnel is to ask, "So, why do you think it didn't work?" Simple and to the point. It will get them to explain from their perspective why they have not been able to get what they need. If you listen closely, you should be hearing some emotional tonality in their voice. Now is the time to help them discover the impact.

"How much do you think that has cost you?" This is the impact question. The answer you are listening for is how much is this costing them in terms of time, money, or other resources. The question you ask to uncover this information should, again, be contextually appropriate and related to the previous answers you have been hearing as you progress through the Pain Funnel.

You might say, "I think I heard you say that they tried to fix it three times—unsuccessfully. I'm wondering, how much has that cost you?" Another appropriate question could be, "So how much time did it take before you realized that they weren't going to be able to fix the problem?" Many times, the prospect has not realized just how much the problem is costing them. When you can get them to verbalize how much money or time they have already spent, it will tend to increase their understanding of the impact and how much it is affecting them.

"How do you feel about that?" The answer to this question will tell you whether their compelling emotional reason (pain) is strong enough to get them to buy your product, service, idea, or solution. What you want to help them discover is how they feel about the impact the problem is having on them. This gets to the emotional connection. Often you will be able to observe the other person and realize that they are emotionally involved with the problem, reason, and impact. When people are emotionally involved, their voice gets louder, they stand up, their face may flush red; other times their voice gets softer, they slump, their face may blanche.

When you observe an emotional reaction, you do not need to literally ask them, "How do you feel about that?" Simply confirm what you are observing. "You look really upset about this." "You seem to be bummed out with all of this." "I get the feeling that you are really excited about this opportunity." These are all good statements to confirm what you have just observed, but you must follow the statement up with a question like, "Is it just me, or are you really feeling that way?" People will usually answer and expand on how and why they are feeling the way they do.

> People buy emotionally and justify
> the decision intellectually.

If you are having a conversation about some issue or opportunity and the other person is not exhibiting any signs of being emotionally connected, we strongly suggest that you address your observation. You can ask, "Maybe it is just me, but why am I getting the feeling that this issue is not that important to you?"

Dave was talking with a vice president of sales whose problem was that his salespeople were not asking for enough referrals. As Dave guided him through the Pain Funnel, he discovered that the VP was the real problem. The reason his team was not getting more referrals was because he had not communicated to them that this was what he wanted them to do and he had not required it to become part of their behavior. Starting with the impact question, here is how the conversation unfolded.

Dave: "So, if your team did ask for more referrals, about how much do you think that would bring in per month in new sales?"

VP: "Oh, probably a million dollars." (This was a large company.)

Dave: "I get the feeling that is not a lot of money in your world?"

VP: "We spend that much a month on paperclips."

Obviously, he was not emotionally involved. Dave found out later that he had given his two-week notice and was moving on to a new company. Even though there is a huge impact, it does not always mean they have their own pain, their own compelling emotional reason. To finish the story, Dave's final question to him was, "So, to whom in the company would a million dollars a month be important?"

A final thought on impact. It is not always money. It could be loss of time, relationships, or opportunity. Listen carefully to what the other person is saying and choose the appropriate impact questions.

- "How much of your time does that require?"
- "It's not keeping you from attending your daughter's gymnastics, is it?"
- "Your spouse is not being affected by all the hours you are putting in to fix this, are they?"

As you become proficient in using the Pain Funnel as a

template for the important conversations in your business, do not be surprised if many times the answers to questions like those above begin a new Pain Funnel. Note that it often takes three or more pains to get them to change from what they currently are doing.

"Have you given up trying to deal with the problem?" The answer to this question will determine and confirm if they are willing to fix the problem or to seize the opportunity. (Remember, compelling emotional reasons can be pain or gain.) How you frame the actual question to get the answer you are looking for needs be contextually and situationally appropriate. There will be times when the literal question, "Have you given up trying to deal with the problem?" is appropriate. However, more often than not, it is easier to get the answer you are looking for, which is a "Yes, I have given up" or a "No, I have to fix this," when you report back to them the summary of all the other Pain Funnel questions.

> **You:** "I think I heard you say that you are sick and tired of putting up with late deliveries, which cause your production line to shut down and which cost you tens of thousands of dollars. You're missing your daughter's gymnastics, and your spouse is upset with the extra time you are spending at the plant. Are we on the same page?"

Them: "Yes, absolutely! And now that I am thinking about it, the cost might be greater." (If this were a real conversation, you could start a new Pain Funnel by asking, "What do you mean, 'greater'?")

You: "It sounds like you have decided to put an end to it by firing your current supplier and finding another source. Is that where you are?"

Them: "Yes! I can't keep running my business like this and expect to be successful."

You: "I understand."

A good pain conversation will help them discover that you could be the bridge to get them across the pain crevice, from where they are to where they want to be. Be sure to give this pain conversation enough time to cover everything. The other person should be doing most of the talking during this step in the conversation. That means it will take longer than just you showing up and telling them about your great products or services.

Revenue Generation Step 3: The Investment Conversation

Now that you have determined the other person has enough pain, you must determine if they are willing and able to invest what it will take to fix it. What could the investment be? The first thing most of us think of is money, but it could also be time, people, other resources, or a combination of any of the above. The purpose of this step is to find out if they are willing and able to make the required investment.

Revenue generation for your business requires others to spend money for your product or service. Too many solopreneurs begin by providing too many unpaid or discounted services. To generate revenue, stick to your price for your product or service. But remember, not everyone will be your prospective customer or client. Part of the conversation must determine how much they are willing and able to pay. If everyone you talk to is buying what you're selling, your price is too low. If no one is buying what you're selling, your price is too high.

Start the investment conversation by reviewing what you learned while discovering their compelling emotional reason to buy. If you fail to review their pain, the investment conversation can quickly turn into an intellectual arm-wrestling contest. So, let's play out a possible investment conversation.

You: "So when it comes to fixing this late-delivery issue that is costing you nearly a million dollars per year and is keeping you from your daughter's gymnastics, I am curious how much more per unit your budget can handle to get better delivery."

Them: "Well, we could probably handle another 1 or 2% without upsetting our customers."

You: "OK. So how much would that be per unit?"

Them: "We spend about $27 now. I am thinking maybe $27.50."

You: "That's interesting. What if I told you that to guarantee 99% on-time delivery, it could take the price up to as much as $32? Would we still be talking?"

Them: "Wow, that's pretty pricey!"

You: "I understand. My hope is that it would not be that much, but if it is, I don't want you to be surprised. Let's figure out if it even makes sense for you. You said earlier in the conversation that you use an average of 45,000 units per year, correct?"

Them: "Yeah, that's pretty accurate."

You: "OK, then, grab your calculator and let's put in these numbers: 45,000 × $27. Is that pretty close to what you have been spending per year for your units?"

Them: "Yep, right on it."

You: "And how much was that total?"

Them: "$1,215,000."

You: "Now put in these numbers: 45,000 × $32. What total do you get?"

Them: "$1,440,000."

You: "Now subtract $1,215,000 from that $1,440,000, and what do you get?"

Them: "$225,000."

You: "So, it seems that up to an additional $225,000 should be able to stop the annual million-dollar loss and get you to your daughter's gymnastics. Now the only question you need to answer is, if required, are you willing and able to make that type of investment or not?"

> Have them do the math or punch the numbers into the calculator. People will believe their numbers before they believe your numbers.

While engaging in the kind of conversation above, be sure to wind up with a number that will be higher than what your price will be. This allows you to come in less than what they were expecting and will build trust and confidence in working with you. Use this investment conversation to manage their expectations.

This is not the only way to engage in an investment conversation. You can begin with simple inquiries like, "What budget have you set aside for this?" "What are you currently investing?" "Where would the money come from to pay for a project like this?" You manage expectations with questions like, "What if that is not enough?" or "If you could only afford a portion of the project, where would you want to start?"

When you can help them figure out if it makes sense to invest in your product or service, you become a trusted advisor rather than just another vendor trying to convince them to buy your product or service. Remember, you must find out if they are willing and able to invest the money, time, and resources. Many people are willing to invest in your product or service but are not able—they don't have any money. Others will have the money but will not be willing to invest in your product or service because they have not discovered that they have a compelling emotional reason to do so. Therefore, the pain conversation about their compelling emotional reasons must occur before you can have a meaningful investment conversation.

Revenue Generation Step 4: Decision Making

Can they and will they be able to make a decision? Find out before you waste time, money, and effort creating an awesome presentation that you present to people who can't or won't make a decision. It is key to uncover the decision process. This will allow you to understand their process and to decide if you want to pursue them or not.

There are several key points to uncover when engaged in a conversation about the process they will go through to decide whether to buy your product or service. *Who, what, how, when, where*, and *why* questions all need to be answered by the prospective buyer.

Who: It is important to know who besides themselves will be involved. Find out if they are collecting information for some other person who will decide, if they will consult others, or if they just have to "bounce" it off someone else. Once you find out who else that might be, find out why that person is involved. Often, they will tell you, "No one but me!" If they tell you there is no other decision maker but themselves, be brave enough to ask this question: "There must be a reason no one else is involved. Why is that?" As they answer, they confirm to themselves that they are willing and able to decide.

What: You will gain valuable information by asking your

prospect what process they go through to arrive at their decision. We once talked to a company about training their ten salespeople. The *what* conversation went something like this:

Us: "Felix, when it comes to deciding whether to invest nearly $100,000 to improve your sales team's ability to close more business, I am curious. What process will you go through to decide whether or not to actually do it?"

Felix: "Well, you know, I am talking with four other companies."

Us: "Of course, I understand. But how are you going to decide which one of us to actually use to help your salespeople?"

Felix: "Obviously, I am meeting with each of you. Then I will ask at least three of you to make a presentation and share all your content so that I can see exactly what you will be teaching my people. I will then have two of you come back and present a one-day overview of your program to the sales team, then have both trainers meet with each of my people for about an hour, and then provide a written summary of what you think of each of my people. I will then ask each of them who they would like to work with, and if we get a unanimous vote, that's who we'll choose."

At this point we had enough information to decide if this is the kind of client we wanted to work with or not. He was asking for a lot of free access to our material and our time, and then the decision was based on who his team would choose. This didn't seem like a game we wanted to play. We ended up telling him our process for bringing on clients, which was decidedly different than what he had in mind. We politely decided not to do business together. We learned later from one of the trainers who made the cut that the owner ended up not engaging with anyone but created a program of bits and pieces from the two trainers who had done the day-long overviews and the summaries of what his sales team needed. We highly advise against unpaid consulting.

> There is no wrong decision process, just one in which you may choose to not participate.

How: Be sure to understand how the decision is made. Some people will say, "If I like it, I buy it." Others will say, "If the data supports what we need, we buy it." Don't be surprised to hear, "Everyone affected by the decision votes and the majority decides." Once you understand what the process is and how they come to a decision, make sure to provide the information required for them to engage in their process so they are able to make a decision. But only provide that information at the right time and to the right people. The complexity of your product or service and the length of your sales cycle will determine when to share the appropriate information. This will also be affected by their answers to the *when* question below.

When: Many people attempt to find out when the prospect will decide by asking directly, "When will you make your decision on which vendor you choose?" But this creates too much pressure. We advise you to start with the end in mind. Take them to a place in the future when they are consuming or using your product or service, then work backwards. This forces them to create the urgency of when the decision needs to be made. Try something like this.

> **You:** "Let's pretend that you selected your new supplier and you are ready to begin installing the new units. What date are you looking at in the future?"

> **Them:** "Well, we only have room for one week of inventory and we are committed to three more weeks from our current supplier, so I am guessing it is about four weeks from now."

> **You:** "So if I hear you correctly, you run out of the current inventory in four weeks, so you want to begin us-

ing the new supplier's units five weeks from today?"

Them: "Yep, that would be ideal."

You: "That might be a problem. The typical delivery window, from order to your plant, is 14 days. So, your first order would have to be placed three weeks from now. It typically takes 10 to 14 days to get all the paperwork in place to start working together. If you take those two weeks into account, that means you would need to decide on your new vendor in the next day or two. That's probably putting too much pressure on you, isn't it?"

This allows them to discover that to solve the problem they have to make a decision more quickly than they may have anticipated, and it keeps you from sounding like a pushy salesperson constantly asking for the decision. Knowing when they need to begin using your product or service will allow you to decide if you can deliver within their constraints.

Where: As you engage in a decision-making conversation, be sure to find out where the decision is going to be made. This will typically apply when you are talking to larger companies or when there are multiple decision makers. Find out where, both hierarchically within their organization and geographically, the final decision is made. Even though you asked if others are involved, by asking at what level in the company the final approval is required, they will give you a position. Every position in a company has a person who performs the responsibilities of that position. The person you are talking to may believe they make the decision but will often forget to tell you that their decision needs the approval of the company's COO, who happens to be in Stuttgart, Germany. Knowing this information will help you adjust the timeline of when your pseudo-decision maker needs to make their choice.

Revenue Generation Step 5: What Will Happen Next?

The three previous steps, two through four, are the qualifying steps. They can also be thought of as the *dis*qualifying steps. Pendulum theory requires that you qualify an opportunity by attempting to disqualify. If you are unable to disqualify them, you have a great prospect. They have convinced you that they have a strong compelling emotional reason (pain) to buy your product or service, they are willing and able to spend the money on your product or service, and their decision process is something you are willing to engage in. You should now have a qualified prospect. But to be sure, use the concept of mutual agreement to ensure everyone is on the same wavelength. When there is agreement on pain, investment, and decision process, the next mutual agreement is to decide what will happen next.

You: "Let me make sure I have this correct. You are sick and tired of the late deliveries, which could cost you nearly $1 million, and upset because you are missing your daughter's gymnastics. If you had to, you would spend up to $32 per unit but would prefer to keep in as close to the $27 as possible. And finally, as the owner of the company, this is your decision to make with input from your plant manager so that you can start using the new units in the production runs starting 4–5 weeks from now. Have I missed anything?"

Them: "No, you are right on track. Seems like you have a grasp on what we need."

You: "Good. From your perspective, what do you think our next step should be?"

Them: "Well, isn't this where you give us a proposal or a quote?"

You: "That certainly seems like the logical next step, and I am happy to do that. It will take me a couple of days to get everything together and make sure we have everything on our end. Can we go ahead and schedule time to make our presentation to you and the plant manager in the next three days or so?"

Them: "No problem. Next Tuesday at the same time as today will work for us."

You: "OK, I have that in my book. We will present our solution to you, and if you don't like it for any reason, are you OK just telling me?"

Them: "You can be assured that I have no problem telling you no!"

You: "I appreciate that. Now, let's pretend we answer all your questions, and you love our solution. What would happen then?"

Them: "Well, at that point we would welcome you as our new vendor!"

You: "And if you can't, or don't want to do that, you will tell me, right?"

Them: "Absolutely!"

You: "Sounds like I had better get started on that proposal."

This is an example of achieving clarity on the next step. Notice how the above used the concept of mutual agreements? You got them to decide what the next step should be and agreed to it. You achieved mutual agreement on what would happen if they didn't like your proposal and what would happen if they did.

Do not agree to anything unless you know what is going to happen if you do.

When you get the other person to suggest what should happen next, they feel as if it is their idea. By always providing the option of telling you no if there is not a fit, you alleviate any pressure they may feel about you attempting to "sell" them. If it is their idea, with no pressure, they will always be more predisposed to you and your product or service.

The next step is not always a proposal or presentation. Often it is having another meeting with other individuals or a meeting to acquire needed information. You should find this out in the decision-process step, and it should be confirmed with what they tell you the next step should be. Remember, there is no wrong decision process, just one you may choose not to participate in. But if you do choose to participate, follow their process and provide everything they need to make their decision.

Revenue Generation Step 6: Here Is What I Can Do for You

People want and need to know what is in it for them. This is the step in the conversation when you share with them how your product or service will solve their pain, within their budget, and in accordance with their decision process. This part of the conversation can take place at the end of a half-hour meeting when all the previous steps have been discussed, or it could happen after the fifth meeting. The point is to ensure that you understand the other person's situation and that you or your product can help them solve whatever it is they need to have solved.

Always begin this part of the conversation with a review of what you understand their situation to be. This should include their pains, investment, decision process, and what they indicated would happen if they like your solution. After the review, present what you can do for them to solve their issues.

It is this simple. The problem most salespeople have is that they want to do this step first, without understanding the other person and their situation. If you have the belief (trap) that your product or service will sell itself, you run the risk of "showing up and throwing up" all the wonderful features and benefits of your great product or service, only one of which is of interest to them. We have a rule we teach our clients: "Don't spill your candy in the lobby." Take the time to understand which specific kind of candy the other person likes, then give just that candy to them.

When you follow the previous five steps, you will know what the other person is looking for and what they truly need. Whether your explanation of what you can do for them is a 5-minute explanation of your product or service or a 100-page proposal, the point is to ensure it is tailored to their wants and needs for their reasons. Based on your mutual agreement, the other person will likely tell you yes or no after you have presented your solutions and answered all their questions.

Revenue Generation Step 7: The Next Step Forward

Once you get to this point, ask what they want to do next. If the prior steps have been done properly, most of the time the prospect will say they want to buy your product or service. On some occasions, they will say no. Let's deal with the *no* first.

When you come this far and get the *no*, it is also time to get the lesson. Why did they say no? Odds are that you did not do one of the previous steps well. Let them know that you appreciate them telling you no, but ask why and listen to their answer. Take the time to debrief where you went wrong. Work back from this step. Did you do a good "what will happen next?" step? If so, how good was the decision-making step? Perhaps you didn't understand their process. If that step was good, what about the investment conversation? Did you do more than ask if they had a budget? And finally, how good was your "compelling emotional reason" step? By working backwards, you can determine where the conversation may have broken down, get your lesson, and fix it so there is less chance of it happening next time.

But even if they say, "Yes, let's get started!" the sales conversation is not over. You must be clear on the next step forward. You must obtain mutual agreement on what going forward means. Let us give you an example of how this conversation may unfold.

You: "So you want to start purchasing our units?"

Them: "Absolutely. I like your plan for how we would order and your just-in-time delivery options."

You: "OK. This is what going forward means. First, we will need to get all the paperwork and credit reports completed and on file. Then we will need to work with you on getting that first order together so we can deliver by the date you requested. Does that make sense to you?"

Them: "Yes, of course."

You: "Our experience is that changing vendors can sometimes cause bumps in the road as the change is being made. If you or your people have any issues as we make this change, would you agree to call me immediately so I can minimize any impact on you?"

Them: "Sure, that makes sense."

You: "If my team is experiencing any bumps from our perspective, is it OK if I reach out to you to minimize any impact?"

Them: "Absolutely!"

This conversation should be as detailed as needed to assure them that there will be minimal surprises, but also include that if one should arise, here's how it will be handled. Tell them what you are going to be doing to them and with them so there is no mutual mystification. Now that they are a customer, be sure they know what to expect and what to do if their expectations are not being met.

Increasing revenue should be one of the goals of all business owners. Increasing revenue will occur when you have similar conversations to the ones we share in this book with your potential customers. But also, more effective and efficient conversations with your employees can make them more productive and potentially increase revenue. Think of your interactions with prospects, customers, employees, and vendors as conversations about the truth between adults. When you follow the conversation template we share in this book, you are seeking to understand the other person and are being mindful of the context and situation. This should ensure more positive outcomes.

Gate Selling

You now have a template for revenue generating conversations, especially the sales conversations. Knowing when and for which parts of the sales process to use them is part of a good revenue generation process. For every business owner who reads this book, there is a different process in which they sell their products or services. You may have a product or service that you can sell in a one-call conversation, or you may have to make multiple calls and engage in multiple conversations. Figure out the normal process your company and your buyer must complete before you sell them your product or service.

This is something you'll need to do whether you are an interior design firm for homeowners or a small manufacturer providing jet airplane parts to a huge aerospace company. The details of the process are essential. What information must you acquire from your prospective customer before you are able to provide them with a proposal? How many different people will you need to contact? What are the steps you go through to sell what your company offers? Create the process you go through with your prospective customers and include everything you need to know in each step.

The following is a simple example of what we call Gate Selling.

Gate 1	Gate 2	Gate 3
Initial Qualification	Technical Information Gathering	Present, Answer Questions, and Close

♦ Discover their pain
♦ Uncover the budget
♦ Understand their decision process
♦ Up-front contract for next meeting
	♦ Review pain, budget, and decision process
	♦ Review all technical requirements
	♦ Discuss any options for change
	♦ What will happen next?
		♦ Review pain, budget, and decision process
		♦ Here is what I can do for you
		  ◊ Presentation
		♦ Next step forward
		  ◊ Up-front contract now that they are customers

You always start at Gate 1 and do not move to Gate 2 until all the requirements of Gate 1 are met. You stay in Gate 2 until you get everything you need, and then you move to Gate 3. There could be a few gate cycles, as in the example we've shared above, or there could be lots of them in a more complex sale with multiple decision makers. It all depends on the sales cycle that matches up with your target market. The point is, there are a number of unique gates that have to be encountered in order, and these gates must incorporate all the elements of the 7-Step Template for Revenue Generation. No jumping ahead! Create as many or as few gates as you need to take the opportunity from the first conversation all the way to becoming a customer or client.

Please note that we recommend that you always review the prospective buyer's pain (the business problem that is keeping them up at night), budget (available resources for solving the problem), and decision process (what must happen before there is a commitment to work together). It's quite important to ask if anything has changed in any of these areas before you make a formal recommendation. If something has changed, you need to find out what has changed and how it affects the path you and this person are planning to take. You might need to make changes to a proposal or plan for another person to be involved in the final decision.

You may have guessed by now that it's our thinking that no one likes to be surprised. Make sure you stay on top of what is expected of you and your expectations of them, and deal with any changes.

SUMMARY OF KEY POINTS

Get ready for your day off!

- Set revenue generation as a strategic priority.
- Learn and use the 7-Step Template for Revenue Generation.
- Create the process you go through with your prospective customers, including everything you need to know to get through each gate of the sales process.

CHAPTER 8

Alignment

This chapter gives you the antidote for Trap 8: "I'm Not a Natural-Born Salesperson," along with additional tactics for dealing with the dysfunctional beliefs behind each of the nine traps we have examined in this book.

Why Skill Is Not Enough

There are many components of success. Now that you realize business ownership requires you to be consciously selling without being "salesy," you can increase revenue by improving your skills. However, skill alone will not win the day. There are three key areas to constantly and consistently improve upon if your aim is to run a successful business and lead a successful life. These are behavior, technique, and attitude. When you can align these critical components, increased success soon follows. Taken together, they are known as the Success Triangle.

Behavior

Let's pretend that you are a solopreneur—your business is just you. You must create your product or service, which is a behavior. You must attend to the accounting details, which is a behavior. You must do the marketing, which is a behavior. Often, you must take out the trash, which is a behavior. The point is to highlight all the various things you must do to successfully grow your business. As you grow and hire employees, many of these tasks can be delegated to them.

Behavior is what you do to achieve your goals. Any goal that you set for yourself or your business, when broken down, will require you to do something. The goal that does not require anything of you is a dream, hope, or wish. If your goal is to keep a clean production area, then you could be the janitor, which means what you will be doing is taking out the trash, cleaning all the surfaces, and mopping the floors. The other option is to hire a cleaning service, which means what you will be doing is making calls, interviewing services, and writing the check to pay the cleaning service you chose. You get the idea—there will always be something you have to do to achieve the goal.

If increasing revenue is the goal, what will you have to do? Lack of clarity of the specific behaviors required to increase revenue is the downfall of many failed ventures. Take a moment in your working document and list as many behaviors as you can think of that allow you to increase revenue.

> Behave your way to success.

Many lists include things like "ask for referrals," "post blogs or vlogs in social media," "buy advertising," "go on sales calls," "improve production efficiency," "raise prices," "make cold calls," "hire a salesperson," "fire a salesperson," and the list goes on. Knowing what you need to do to get what you say you want is the first step to success. We like to keep a little note posted at our desks that says: "Now that you know it, act like it." Just because you know what you need to do, it is not enough. You have to actually do it! Behaving your way to success requires articulating a goal, identifying the behaviors you must do to achieve that goal, and mustering the discipline to do the behaviors.

Choose the three or four behaviors that you believe will have the most impact on increasing revenues, and do them on a regular, consistent basis. If you need to ask customers for more referrals, block time every week in your calendar to do just that specific behavior. Decide on how many times you will ask for referrals each week. Do not worry about the outcome of whether you get a referral; concentrate on doing the specific behavior in the time you have set aside.

Technique

Behavior becomes technique (the second point on the Success Triangle) once the conversation begins. Making the virtual call or the phone call is the behavior; what you say once the other person is listening to you is technique.

Technique is the *how* of doing something. The *what* is the 7-Step Template for Revenue Generation; the *how* was in the examples we shared. Like any skill set, technique requires practice, repetition, and a good coach.

One of our co-workers is skilled at woodcarving. He is truly a woodcarving artist at an elite level. He shared with us that he has a woodcarving coach. As good as he is, he wants to get better. He told us that his coach will constantly push him to improve his technique and give him tips on how to refine his already outstanding work.

Our point is to urge you to constantly refine your technique in all the business ownership skills, not just increasing revenue. If this sounds like shameless self-promotion to get a Sandler coach, we are OK with that. The purpose of this book is to help you increase revenue by realizing that you are, in fact, selling. No one is a born salesperson. Professional sales skills require modern sales techniques, ongoing reinforcement, and refinement of your revenue generating conversations. A good coach will help you stay focused.

In the behavior example of asking for referrals, what you say and how you say it is important. Part of your mutual agreement with a customer should be that you will ask for referrals from time to time. If they agree, put them on your list of customers to call for referrals.

Say you're a graphic designer with some very happy clients. The next hour in your calendar is booked to call customers for referrals, so you pick up the phone, call your first customer on today's list, and say, "Hey, Javier, this is Allison over at ABC Designs. Do you have any referrals for me?" You did the behavior, which is better than not doing it, but your technique could use some polish. Start with checking in on how they are doing, remind them of your mutual agreement about referrals, and create a story before you ask for the actual referral. It could sound like this.

Allison: "Hi, Javier. This is Allison just checking in. How is business going?"

Javier: "Hey, Allison. Good to hear from you. Business is going great. In fact, we are having a record-breaking year!"

Allison: "Wow, that is great to hear. It's not because of that great new graphic on your packaging is it?" [Laughs.]

Javier: "I am sure that has helped. I am also giving credit to that new salesperson we hired. She is bringing in new clients every week."

Allison: "Happy to hear things are going well. Speaking of new clients, I am on a mission myself to bring in some new ones. Remember when we agreed that I would ask for referrals from time to time?"

Javier: "Sure do."

Allison: "So this is that time. I noticed that your foursome won the charity golf scramble a few weeks ago.

I was wondering, if you were me doing what I do, who in that group would you call first about needing design help?"

Javier: "Funny you would mention it. Georgia was talking about how tired her marketing material was looking. So, I guess I would call her first."

Allison: "That makes sense. Would you be comfortable reaching out to her, giving her a little background of what we have done for your company, and asking her if she would entertain a call from me? I like to do it this way so that I am only calling if she wants me to. Would you be comfortable with that?"

Javier: "Absolutely. I am happy to help you out. Give me about a week to reach her and get back with you."

Allison: "Sounds like a plan. Thank you for helping."

This type of approach is more conversational and will create better results. Just a note on referrals—referrals are a two-way street. If you will be asking for referrals, be sure that you are actively giving referrals.

Knowing what to say and how to say it is a never-ending process of mastery. Technique that worked yesterday may not be as effective tomorrow. Two of the best skills you can develop are to listen and to ask appropriate questions at the right time.

> Two of the best skills you can develop are to listen and to ask appropriate questions at the right time.

Listening skills require the ability to understand what the other person is saying. This means you must pay attention to more than just the words. As we discussed earlier in the book, the other person's behavioral style, physiology, and tonality all give you clues to their true meaning. To stay focused on the other person's message, it is helpful if you give up your need to be right and put your ego on the shelf. Do your best to communicate from a Nurturing Parent and Adult ego state. Waiting for them to take a breath so you can get your point across would not qualify as an excellent listening technique. Listen to understand.

If you listen to understand, you will probably ask questions to clarify what they say. This is good technique. But you must not forget to ask the questions we covered in the 7-Step Template for Revenue Generation, including the Pain Funnel. These questions, when asked at the right time and in the appropriate manner, will save you time and generate revenue.

Attitude

Your attitude is either positive or negative; there is no neutral. When you hear the word "salesperson," what goes through your mind—a negative thought or feeling or a positive thought or feeling? When you came to the realization that as a business owner you had to sell, how did you feel—happy or upset? Your answers to these questions reveal your attitude toward sales and salespeople. If your first reaction skews negative on this, our hope is to reframe what and how you think about selling. Most negative associations come from experiences with poor salespeople attempting to convince someone to buy something they don't need or want.

Do you recall our earlier discussion of I/R Theory and comfort zones? How you value yourself is a major factor in your success. The I/R scale is really a measure of the degree of positive or negative attitude you have regarding your core being. Whatever self-talk you have going on between your ears will dictate your level of success. But wait! Throughout this book, we've been talking about many traps. Aren't those traps self-talk? Self-talk regarding things you believe to be true, like thinking your product will sell itself, will not work because the belief has no basis in truth. When you believe the product will sell itself without you having to do anything but produce it, you are indulging in wishful thinking. Your attitude is the positive or negative thoughts going through your mind daily, particularly about yourself and the many roles you experience as a business owner.

Success: Connecting the Points of the Triangle

The three elements we have shared with you in this chapter—behavior, technique, and attitude—are essential for success in any field. Success, in other words, is the result of connecting all the points of the Success Triangle.

One of the best things about success is that you get to define it for yourself. This simple, powerful model has helped well over a million people define and achieve success on their own terms. It can do the same for you and ensure you escape the Revenue Killer "I'm Not a Natural-Born Salesperson" Trap.

SUMMARY OF KEY POINTS

Get ready for your day off!

- Make conscious choices about your behavior. Once you know what you want, act like it.
- Accept that strong technique requires practice, repetition, and a good coach.
- Remember that your attitude is either positive or negative—there is no neutral.

CHAPTER 9

The Owner's Dashboard

This brief chapter points you toward a simple tool you can use to run your business without stressing yourself out—so you can actually take a day off when you need one. It also provides the antidote to the Revenue Killer "Sales Is Just a Numbers Game" Trap.

Are You on Course?

The plans are in action, the positions and functions are defined, and the people are in the correct positions. Whether your company is two people or 80, you are at the helm. You are steering the company toward your company vision. One of the roles of a business owner is to keep the company on course. Much like the pilot of an airplane, you need to constantly check the compass heading to make sure you will land at the correct destination.

How will you make your progress, and your company's progress, visual? What does your instrument panel or dashboard look like? What do you need to monitor on a regular basis to make sure your company is on course?

Key Performance Indicators

Key performance indicators—the ubiquitous KPIs. If your goal is to generate more revenue and the only thing you pay attention to is the quarterly statement of income, you might be disappointed. If the only thing you monitor is daily deposits, you might be adding unnecessary stress. Both are important, but both have weaknesses. Quarterly statements are lagging indicators. By the time you see them, it is too late to make a difference for that quarter. Daily cash flow goes up and down and will cause distress every day it is below expectations. Instead, monitor the leading indicators of revenue growth for your company. What are the indicators that will lead to consistent daily cash flow or to reaching quarterly revenue goals?

The number of revenue generating conversations—talking with people about whether your product or service is a fit for them—is the key leading indicator of how your daily cash flow or quarterly reports will look. This KPI is vital to track on a regular basis even if you are currently the only salesperson. How many sales conversations does it take to generate a sale in your world? If you track this behavior long enough to know your close ratios, you can go to the bank consistently on the results. To get more granular, how many attempts to contact a specific lead (which we call outreaches) does it take to result in a sale? An outreach happens whenever you or a salesperson proactively dial a phone, send a text, or message in social media to a specific person for the purpose of setting up a revenue generating conversation.

When Dave was the only salesperson in his training company, he tracked these behaviors without fail. To get 10 new sales per month, he had to take 12 revenue conversations completely through the 7-Step Template for Revenue Generation. To have 12 revenue conversations, he knew that he had to have 17 first appointments; to get 17 first appointments, he had to talk to 20 new leads. (At that point in Dave's business, most new leads came from referrals.) And finally, to talk to 20 new leads, he had to make 100 outreaches to contact those leads. Because he had tracked these numbers for over ten years, he knew it took 5 outreaches, on average, per day, to contact and talk to a new lead.

The key word here is *talk*. This does not mean send email messages back and forth. This means outreaching for the purpose of having a conversation about scheduling a time to talk further. How many outreaches were made to contact and talk with a new lead was the only thing in Dave's control. He knew that if he made no outreaches, there would be no new revenue generated approximately 30 days later. Turning on his afterburner meant he needed to make those outreaches no matter how he felt.

> It is not how you feel that determines how you behave.
> It is how you behave that determines how you feel.

Another motivator is that Dave knew how much money he made for every outreach, whether the prospect answered the phone, sent the call to voicemail, ignored his text, or booked a sales appointment. Over the years he had tracked the number of sales and the revenue results. His average sale for new business was $32,000 (plus or minus $1,000). This allowed him to figure out that he made $3,200 per outreach to contact a new lead. He also knew that he made more than $18,000 for every first revenue generating conversation he conducted.

The lesson here is to put the leading cause, which you can control, of revenue generation as a KPI on your dashboard. If you track the number of outreaches that you or your salespeople make, you will be able bank on the outcome. It also allows you to catch a slump in the KPI before it is too late.

> Sales is more than a numbers game. It is knowing and tracking the right numbers that are leading indicators of success.

Your dashboard should be simple, visual, and based on the top priorities on which you are currently working. Your dashboard does not replace your monthly or quarterly financial reports. Your dashboard should be what you look at on a daily/weekly basis to make sure you are on track to hit those monthly and quarterly goals.

This is how Dave's daily tracking and dashboard looked.

You can see that Dave's technology was not sophisticated; he just tallied with hash marks. He would total each week and keep a running cumulative total for each month and each quarter.

Attempts	~~HHH~~ ||	
Contacts	||	
Appts Booked	|	
First Appts	|||	
Sales	|	Total $27,320

While the outreaches will be the only thing you can control from a behavior perspective, you can improve results by improving your technique. Over time, the appointments booked and first appointments will level out because the first appointments you go on today were booked several days before. If you notice that first appointments are dropping off from the number of appointments booked, you may have a technique problem during the conversation to book the appointment. Again, this is where a good coach will help you improve your technique.

You will probably need other leading indicators. If your production capabilities cannot keep pace with the number of sales, you have a problem. It is OK to add a daily production number to your daily/weekly dashboard. By tracking these two numbers, over time you will be able to see when an issue could arise. Perhaps production is outpacing sales, which would result in an inventory problem.

Our recommendation is to continue looking at the monthly and quarterly reports and to create a weekly/monthly dashboard of two to five leading indicators that affect the final numbers so that you can adjust—before it is too late.

Accountability

When it comes to revenue generation, the people in your company responsible for sales should be held accountable for doing the daily behaviors that are within their control. In the example above, that would be the number of outreaches to contact a lead. To be accountable, two things are required: a behavior and someone to be accountable to. To whom is the business owner accountable? A coach will often fill this role, or an extremely disciplined business owner can hold themselves accountable. If you have a salesperson or a sales team, you must hold them accountable to the minimum daily behaviors that have been agreed to.

Dave hates to admit that he is not the most disciplined person in the world. While running his small training business, he had to trap himself into doing the right daily behaviors—he is easily distracted by the purple squirrels. Dave decided that he would reward himself with one video game at the end of the workday if all his daily behavior was accomplished. If he was able to complete his daily behavior each day for a week, he allowed himself the enjoyment of going to the theater to watch a new movie (his wife is not a movie person). If all the daily behavior was accomplished for the entire month, he would take her out to a nicer-than-normal restaurant of her choice. So who in that scenario was holding him accountable? Of course, his wife! Every day she would check in to make sure he was on track.

If you find that one of your salespeople is not doing the minimum daily behaviors and you have worked with them to improve but they still do not do the behaviors, make sure you have a mutual agreement with them about the process of self-selecting out of your company. The process should have one or two consequences prior to them leaving. The first time you must talk with them about performing, be sure to let them know what the result will be of a second conversation, such as the loss of commission points or base salary. If there is a third conversation, it will be an exit interview.

In the positions section of this book, we discussed having a job description for each function in your company. Each of those job descriptions should have a minimum daily performance expectation. For your company to maximize revenue and minimize expenses, hold employees accountable for performing the expected minimum daily behaviors and make sure you have a conversation with them about consequences. It is better to have mutual agreements rather than surprises. If you yourself have trouble completing your minimum daily behaviors, find someone who will hold you accountable, like a spouse, partner, or coach.

SUMMARY OF KEY POINTS

Get ready for your day off!

- Make your progress, and your company's progress, visual.
- Identify key performance indicators that connect to your top priorities.
- Track leading and lagging measurements of success.
- Find someone who will hold you accountable.

CHAPTER 10

Knowing
to Owning

When we first met Avery at the beginning of our book, she was at a tipping point. She was entering her fourth year in business and doing well fiscally, but she was nearing burnout.

Avery's interior design firm had three employees who helped fulfill project requirements, but she was the primary source for new business growth. Her projects were getting larger and more profitable. The prior year, she had been thrilled to win three large and prestigious projects. Naturally, she focused most of her efforts on client service and delivery. The projects were nearing completion, ribbon cuttings were scheduled, and everything was on track to be a complete success.

As the CEO, Avery was proud of the work she and her team had done for the client and optimistic about the future. She believed that with such prestigious projects now on her firm's resume and a renewed marketing plan underway, prospective new clients would be seeking her out. She was a natural at building relationships, so closing new business should have been easier now. But while sometimes it was, too often it wasn't.

She was tired of submitting preliminary designs (free consulting) to prospective clients and finding that she was stuck trying to differentiate her beautiful design from her competitor's beautiful design. While still feeling the sting of a loss from one particularly frustrating and time-consuming response for proposal process, Avery began asking herself some hard questions:

- Why had she committed so much of the firm's time and resources to the project?
- What evidence did she have to support her belief that she would win?
- What could she have missed?
- Why did she win some clients and lose others?
- Why did some projects seem to move to contract quickly and others seemed to drag on for far too long?
- Why was her business and her cash flow still unpredictable?

She decided it was time to do something different and reached out to us for help. We discovered that Avery was relying so heavily on her natural ability to build relationships that she did not have a framework for walking prospective clients from first meeting to contract. She had no consistent way of identifying clients who were a good fit for her areas of brilliance. Equally as important, she had no way of quickly evaluating opportunities that were not a good fit. This prevented her from investing her energy and effort in opportunities where she could win.

Avery took the first step and began to implement the strategies we've described in this book. She reconnected with her passion. She developed a framework for identifying the right opportunities for her company and saying no to the wrong ones. She developed a habit of investing her time in her highest and best use activities, delegating, or simply saying no to the rest. Soon she had an efficient and effective framework for her selling conversations, and her pipeline became robust and predictable. She hired a full-time marketing person and added more designers. She decided that she would continue to be the primary source of revenue for her company. Much to her surprise, she actually liked selling!

You might be wondering if that's only true for the small-business owner. Consider Ruben. When he first met with us, he had already had a successful career as CEO of publicly and privately held corporations. He was now CEO of a life science start-up with about 25 employees. They had developed a truly revolutionary product that would save people who, otherwise, would die from a disease with no cure. That seems easy right? Who does not dream of representing a product that cures a fatal disease? Of course, doctors want to save patients. This should be a slam dunk!

Sadly, in the life science space, a lot of truly life-saving products never make it to mainstream patient care because their funding runs out before their sales numbers achieve marketability. As we learned early, "better" does not guarantee success. Ruben was keenly aware that people would die without this product and that he had a responsibility to create a return on investment for the shareholders.

The investors were becoming impatient and asking tough questions.

- Why were the top 20% of Ruben's salespeople making their goals, but they could not accurately predict which deals would close or when?
- Why couldn't the underperforming salespeople just do the same things as the top 20%?

Ruben had hired smart and ambitious salespeople. Their markets had been carefully selected with hospitals that possessed the ideal patient profile and catchment area. The product was literally a lifesaver. Sure, it required a capital investment, but they could prove the return on investment for the hospital. What was wrong?

Ruben realized that he had a stringent, repeatable process for every department in his company—except selling. We began to work with him to build a framework for the selling process. We created a playbook that clearly defined each gate in their selling process and carefully defined the Go/No-Go criteria for committing resources to each gate. His salespeople learned to establish relationships based on equal business stature with prospective buyers, who were elite surgeons and executives operating at the highest levels of leadership in the hospitals. This formula separated his salespeople from their competitors and ensured the success of the hospital and the patient. It took guts and determination but paid off. Two short years later, Ruben's company sold for north of $100 million. Ruben is still out doing what he loves and saving lives.

Many of the concepts we've shared seem like common sense. But knowledge alone of these concepts is not enough; application requires a plan and disciplined practice. As we've said before, you must do what you have learned. No one ever went from couch potato to marathon runner by simply amassing tons of knowledge. To run a marathon requires application of the knowledge—it requires actually running. Any marathon runner will tell you that they did not complete those 26.219

miles by accident. They will also tell you it's not easy. It requires discipline, and you will endure some discomfort.

The legendary Green Bay Packers coach, Vince Lombardi, put it this way: "The price of success is hard work, dedication to the job at hand, and the determination that whether we win or lose, we have applied the best of ourselves to the task at hand."

> Knowledge alone is not enough;
> application and skill development require
> a plan and disciplined practice.

Avery's business didn't grow simply because she gained some new knowledge. Likewise, Ruben did not have a magic wand that gave his salespeople the skill and the courage they needed to be successful. Both entrepreneurs are thriving today because they took ownership of their roles and were willing to execute on the tactics and strategies they learned. Both leaders invested their time to learn new behaviors. They chose different paths to success. Avery chose to generate revenue through her direct efforts. Ruben chose to generate revenue indirectly by supporting his salespeople. Both took ownership of their leadership role and its revenue generation priority. Coaching got them all the way there.

Like Avery and Ruben, you get to define success on your terms. Apply the principles in this book, and work with a coach if that makes sense to you. Engage your afterburner to generate more revenue, and see if you can't rediscover your weekends.

Go lead! And if you need help along the way, visit us at Sandler.com.

SUMMARY OF KEY POINTS

Get ready for your day off!

- Move from knowing to owning through practice.
- Reach out to us at Sandler.com for help along the way.

Look for these other books on shop.sandler.com:

SALES SERIES

The Art and Skill of Sales Psychology
Asking Questions the Sandler Way
Bootstrap Selling the Sandler Way
Call Center Success the Sandler Way
The Contrarian Salesperson
Digital Prospecting
Gold Medal Selling
LinkedIn the Sandler Way

Prospect the Sandler Way
Retail Success in an Online World
Sandler Enterprise Selling
The Sandler Rules
The Unapologetic Saleswoman
Why People Buy
*You Can't Teach a Kid to
Ride a Bike at a Seminar*

MANAGEMENT & LEADERSHIP SERIES

Change the Sandler Way
Customer Service the Sandler Way
The Intentional Sales Manager
Lead When You Dance
*Motivational Management
the Sandler Way*
Making the Climb
Misery to Mastery
The Right Hire

The Road to Excellence
The Sales Coach's Playbook
The Sandler Rules for Sales Leaders
The Success Cadence
*Transforming Leaders
the Sandler Way*
Winning from Failing
21st Century Ride Along
Scaling Sales Success

PROFESSIONAL DEVELOPMENT SERIES

Accountability the Sandler Way
*From the Board Room to
the Living Room*
Goal-Setting Boot Camp

Negotiating From the Inside Out
Sandler Success Principles
Succeed the Sandler Way

INDUSTRY SERIES

Making Channel Sales Work
Patient Care the Sandler Way
*Selling in Manufacturing
and Logistics*

*Selling Professional Services
the Sandler Way*
*Selling to Homeowners
the Sandler Way*
Selling Technology the Sandler Way